LPIC-1 101-500 V5 EXAM PREP: MASTER LINUX ADMIN WITH 6 PRACTICE TESTS

Realistic Practice Exams with
Detailed Solutions for Success

Ghada Atef

To all aspiring Linux administrators, may this book empower you to conquer the LPIC-1 exam and unlock exciting career opportunities in the world of open-source technology.

"The only limit to our realization of tomorrow will be our doubts of today."

FRANKLIN D. ROOSEVELT

CONTENTS

PREFACE

Welcome to your journey towards mastering Linux administration and achieving your LPIC-1 certification! This book is designed to be your comprehensive guide as you prepare for the 101-500 V5 exam.

Whether you're a seasoned IT professional seeking to expand your skillset or a newcomer eager to enter the world of open-source technology, the LPIC-1 certification offers a valuable foundation in essential Linux administration tasks. This book provides the resources and guidance you need to solidify your understanding of key concepts, reinforce your practical skills, and build the confidence to excel in the exam.

What you'll find inside:

- Six realistic practice exams** designed to simulate the actual exam format and difficulty level. These exams cover all essential exam domains, allowing you to identify your strengths and weaknesses and focus your studies.
- Detailed explanations accompany each practice test question, providing clear insights into the correct answer and the reasoning behind it. This in-depth analysis helps you not only memorize answers but also gain a deeper understanding of the concepts tested.

This book is your partner in success. By dedicating yourself to studying the material, practicing with the included exams, and actively engaging with the concepts, you'll be well-equipped to tackle the LPIC-1 exam with confidence and achieve your Linux administration goals.

Let's embark on this learning adventure together!

PROLOGUE

The digital landscape is constantly evolving, and the demand for skilled Linux administrators is soaring. Linux, known for its stability, security, and versatility, powers a vast array of systems, from personal computers to enterprise servers. Earning the LPIC-1 certification validates your fundamental understanding of Linux administration and opens doors to exciting career opportunities in various industries.

This prologue serves as a glimpse into the world of Linux administration and the journey you're about to embark on. Imagine yourself confidently navigating the terminal, managing users and groups, configuring file systems, and ensuring the smooth operation of Linux systems. This book equips you with the knowledge and practical skills to transform this vision into reality.

As you delve deeper into the chapters, remember that the path to mastering Linux administration is paved with dedication, perseverance, and a thirst for knowledge. Embrace the challenges, celebrate your victories, and never stop learning. This book is your companion on this rewarding journey, offering guidance, support, and the tools you need to succeed.

Prepare to unlock your potential, conquer the LPIC-1 exam, and embark on a rewarding career as a Linux administrator. The adventure begins now!

STAY CONNECTED!

I appreciate your interest in "LPIC-1 101-500 V5 Exam Prep: Master Linux Admin with 6 Practice Tests." I'm here to support you on your journey towards mastering Linux administration and achieving your LPIC-1 certification.

If you have any questions or feedback about the book, please feel free to reach out to me at:

Email: linux.expert.eg@gmail.com

Please note: Due to the volume of inquiries, it may take up to 72 hours for us to respond. I appreciate your patience and understanding.

I wish you the best of luck in your LPIC-1 exam preparation!

PRACTICE TEST ONE - LPIC-1 EXAM 101 VERSION: 5.0

90 questions | 2 hours | 90% correct required to pass

The LPIC-1 Exam 101 Version: 5.0 Practice Test is a comprehensive resource designed to prepare you for the LPIC-1 (Linux Professional Institute Certification) Exam 101. It includes practice questions that mimic the format and content of the actual test. Each **Question** comes with a detailed **Explanation** to help you understand the concepts better. This practice test is an excellent tool to harness the power of Linux and achieve LPIC-1 certification.

Note

The 101 actual exam is a 90-minute exam with 60 multiple-choice and fill-in-the-blank questions.

Question 1:
What is the primary purpose of the BIOS setup utility or UEFI configuration utility?

A) To configure the operating system after installation.

B) To enable and disable integrated peripherals, change hardware settings, and adjust boot order.

(Correct)

C) To manage user accounts and permissions.

D) To install firmware updates for hardware components.

Explanation

The BIOS setup utility or UEFI configuration utility allows users to configure hardware settings, enable/disable peripherals, and adjust boot order among other functions.

Question 2:

Which key is commonly used to access the BIOS setup utility or UEFI configuration utility during system boot?

A) Ctrl

B) F2

(Correct)

C) Alt

D) Shift

Explanation

The key to access the BIOS setup utility or UEFI configuration utility varies but commonly includes keys like Del, F2, or F12.

Question 3:

What command is used to list all devices currently connected to the PCI bus in a Linux system?

A) lsusb

B) lspci

(Correct)

C) lsmod

D) modprobe

Explanation

The lspci command is used to list all devices currently connected to the PCI bus in a Linux system.

Question 4:

What is the primary purpose of a bootloader in the Linux boot process?

A) Execute system initialization scripts

B) Load the kernel into RAM

(Correct)

C) Perform POST (power-on self-test) diagnostics

D) Initialize hardware components

Explanation

The bootloader's main function is to load the operating system kernel into memory (RAM) so that the kernel can start executing.

Question 5:

Which firmware type reads definitions stored in non-volatile memory to execute pre-defined EFI applications?

A) BIOS

B) UEFI

(Correct)

C) GRUB

D) SysVinit

Explanation

UEFI (Unified Extensible Firmware Interface) reads definitions stored in non-volatile memory to execute pre-defined EFI applications, such as bootloaders.

Question 6:

What is the purpose of the EFI System Partition (ESP) in UEFI systems?

A) Store bootloader configuration files

B) Hold the kernel image

C) Contain the BIOS settings

D) Store pre-defined EFI applications

(Correct)

Explanation

The EFI System Partition (ESP) in UEFI systems contains pre-defined EFI applications, including bootloaders.

Question 7:

Which command is used to customize kernel parameters in GRUB on a Linux system?

A) kernel-config

B) grub-customizer

C) grub-mkconfig

(Correct)

D) grub-editenv

Explanation

The `grub-mkconfig` command is used to generate a new GRUB configuration file, including customized kernel parameters.

Question 8:

What is the purpose of runlevel 5 in a SysVinit system?

A) System shutdown

B) Single user mode

C) Multi-user mode with networking

(Correct)

D) System restart

Explanation

Runlevel 5 is equivalent to runlevel 3 (multi-user mode) but includes the graphical mode login.

Question 9:

Which command is used to manually alternate between runlevels in a running SysVinit system?

A) systemctl

B) initctl

C) telinit

(Correct)

D) runlevel

Explanation

The telinit command is used to alternate between runlevels in a SysVinit system.

Question 10:

In a systemd-based system, what command is used to start a service unit?

A) systemctl start

(Correct)

B) systemctl enable

C) systemctl load

D) systemctl initiate

Explanation

The systemctl start command is used to start a service unit in systemd.

Question 11:

What is the default target in a systemd-based system?

A) runlevel0.target

B) multi-user.target

C) graphical.target

(Correct)

D) shutdown.target

Explanation

The default target in a systemd-based system is typically graphical.target.

Question 12:

Which of the following best describes a partition in Linux?

A) A physical device used to store data.

B) A logical subset of a physical disk.

(Correct)

C) A filesystem used for organizing directories.

D) A mount point for external devices.

Explanation

A partition in Linux is a logical subset of a physical disk. It is used to compartmentalize data on the disk, separating different types of information such as operating system data and user data.

Question 13:

What is the purpose of the EFI System Partition (ESP) in Linux?

A) To store boot loaders and kernel images.

(Correct)

B) To contain system logs and temporary files.

C) To provide additional storage space for user data.

D) To manage swap space for memory pages.

Explanation

The EFI System Partition (ESP) is used to store boot loaders and kernel images for operating systems installed on machines based on the Unified Extensible Firmware Interface (UEFI).

Question 14:

Why might it be beneficial to keep the /var directory on a separate partition?

A) To improve system performance.

B) To reduce the risk of filesystem corruption.

(Correct)

C) To ensure compatibility with legacy systems.

D) To provide additional storage space for user data.

Explanation

Keeping the /var directory on a separate partition can help prevent filesystem corruption caused by misbehaved processes writing excessive data to the filesystem.

Question 15:

What is the recommended swap size for a system with 16 GB of RAM, according to Red Hat Enterprise Linux 7 documentation?

A) At least 4 GB

B) Equal to the amount of RAM

C) 1.5 times the amount of RAM

(Correct)

D) Not recommended

Explanation

According to Red Hat Enterprise Linux 7 documentation, for systems with 8-64 GB of RAM, the recommended swap size with hibernation is 1.5 times the amount of RAM.

Question 16:

What is the purpose of a boot loader?

A) To load an operating system kernel and hand over control to it.

(Correct)

B) To manage disk partitions.

C) To allocate memory for system processes.

D) To configure network settings.

Explanation

A boot loader's primary function is to load an operating system kernel and hand over control to it, initializing the hardware and loading the rest of the operating system.

Question 17:

Which boot loader is commonly used in most Linux distributions?

A) LILO

B) GRUB

(Correct)

C) Syslinux

D) BootX

Explanation

GRUB (GRand Unified Bootloader) is commonly used in most Linux distributions as the boot loader.

Question 18:

What is the primary purpose of the Master Boot Record (MBR) on a disk?

A) It contains a table describing the partitions on the disk.

(Correct)

B) It initializes the hardware during the boot process.

C) It loads the operating system kernel.

D) It stores user data.

Explanation

The MBR contains a table describing the partitions on the disk and also bootstrap code, which is the initial bootloader.

Question 19:

Which partitioning scheme introduced to overcome the limitations of MBR?

A) LVM (Logical Volume Manager)

B) GPT (GUID Partition Table)

(Correct)

C) FAT32 (File Allocation Table 32)

D) NTFS (New Technology File System)

Explanation

GPT (GUID Partition Table) was introduced to overcome the limitations of MBR, such as the maximum number of partitions and disk size.

Question 20:

What is the purpose of shared libraries in a Linux system?

A) To embed library code into executable files

B) To dynamically link programs to reusable code

(Correct)

C) To reduce the size of program files

D) To eliminate the need for libraries at run time

Explanation

The correct answer is B) Shared libraries dynamically link programs to reusable code at run time, reducing program size and allowing for efficient resource management.

Question 21:

Which command is used to display the shared library dependencies of a specific program?

A) `ldconfig`

B) `ls`

C) `ldd`

(Correct)

D) `echo`

Explanation

The correct answer is C) The `ldd` command followed by the absolute path to the program is used to display its shared library dependencies.

Question 22:

What naming convention is followed for shared library files?

A) Library name + .so + Version number

(Correct)

B) Library name + .a + Version number

C) Library name + .dll + Version number

D) Library name + .so + Revision number

Explanation

The correct answer is A) Shared library files follow the convention of Library name + .so + Version number, for example, libpthread.so.0.

Question 23:

What is the primary purpose of the Debian Package Tool (dpkg)?

A) To update the package index

B) To manage software packages on Debian-based systems

(Correct)

C) To perform advanced searches in the package index

D) To remove configuration files associated with packages

Explanation

dpkg is the primary utility used to install, configure, maintain, and remove software packages on Debian-based systems.

Question 24:

Which command is used to install a .deb package using dpkg?

A) dpkg -r

B) dpkg -I

C) dpkg -L

D) dpkg -i

(Correct)

Explanation

The "-i" option is used with dpkg to install a .deb package.

Question 25:

What does APT stand for in the context of Debian-based systems?

A) Advanced Package Tool

(Correct)

B) Application Package Tracker

C) Automated Package Transfer

D) Advanced Program Toolkit

Explanation

APT stands for Advanced Package Tool, which is a package management system for Debian-based systems.

Question 26:

What is the purpose of the `rpm` command in Linux?

A) To manage software repositories

B) To install, upgrade, and remove packages

(Correct)

C) To search for packages in online repositories

D) To list available updates for installed packages

Explanation

The `rpm` command is used to manage software packages on Red Hat-based systems. It is primarily used for installing, upgrading, and removing packages.

Question 27:

Which command is used to install a package with `rpm`?

A) `rpm -a PACKAGENAME`

B) `rpm -u PACKAGENAME`

C) `rpm -i PACKAGENAME`

(Correct)

D) `rpm -s PACKAGENAME`

Explanation

The `-i` option with `rpm` is used to install a package.

Question 28:

How can you list all installed packages on a system using `rpm`?

A) `rpm -q`

B) `rpm -l`

C) `rpm -qa`

(Correct)

D) `rpm -p`

Explanation

The `-qa` option with `rpm` is used to query all installed packages.

Question 29:

What does the `yum` command do in Linux?

A) Manages software packages

(Correct)

B) Creates new repositories

C) Compiles source code

D) Generates package metadata

Explanation

The `yum` command is a package manager used for managing software packages on RPM-based systems.

Question 30:

What is virtualization?

A) A technology allowing a hypervisor to run processes containing fully emulated computer systems.

(Correct)

B) A method to directly boot into a virtual machine without relying on an underlying operating system.

C) A process of creating isolated environments for applications to run independently.

D) A technique for dynamically relocating virtual machines from one hypervisor to another.

Explanation

Virtualization is the technology that allows a hypervisor to run processes containing fully emulated computer systems, known as virtual machines.

Question 31:

Which of the following is a Type-1 hypervisor?

A) VirtualBox

B) KVM

C) Xen

(Correct)

D) VMware Player

Explanation

Xen is a Type-1 hypervisor, meaning it does not rely on an underlying operating system to function.

Question 32:

What is a fully virtualized guest?

A) A virtual machine that is aware it is running as a virtual instance.

B) A virtual machine that utilizes paravirtualized drivers for enhanced performance.

C) A virtual machine where the guest is unaware it is running as a virtual instance.

(Correct)

D) A virtual machine that combines both full and paravirtualization techniques.

Explanation

A fully virtualized guest is one where the guest is unaware that it is running as a virtual instance.

Question 33:

What command displays the current working directory in Linux?

A) `dir`

B) `ls`

C) `cwd`

D) `pwd`

(Correct)

Explanation

The correct answer is D) `pwd`. The `pwd` command stands for "print working directory" and displays the current directory path.

Question 34:

Which command is used to print system information including kernel version and hardware architecture?

A) `uname`

(Correct)

B) `kernel`

C) `version`

D) `sysinfo`

Explanation

The correct answer is A) `uname`. The `uname` command with the `-a` option prints system information including kernel name, version, and hardware architecture.

Question 35:

How can you find help documentation for a specific Linux command?

A) `help`

B) `man`

(Correct)

C) `info`

D) `command_help`

Explanation

The correct answer is B) `man`. Using the `man` command followed by the command name provides access to its manual page, which contains detailed documentation.

Question 36:

What is the purpose of the `cat` command in Linux?

A) It is used to count the number of lines in a file.

B) It is used to concatenate files and display the output.

(Correct)

C) It is used to search for patterns within files.

D) It is used to compress files.

Explanation

The correct answer is B) The `cat` command concatenates files and displays the output to the terminal.

Question 37:

Which command is used to display the last 15 lines of a text file named `example.txt`?

A) `head -n 15 example.txt`

B) `tail -n 15 example.txt`

(Correct)

C) `tail -n 5 example.txt`

D) `head -n 5 example.txt`

Explanation

The correct answer is B) The `tail -n 15 example.txt` command will display the last 15 lines of the `example.txt` file.

Question 38:

Which command is used to list files and directories in a detailed long listing format in Linux, including file permissions, ownership, size, and modification time?

A) ls -a

B) ls -l

(Correct)

C) ls -h

D) ls -R

Explanation

The correct answer is B) ls -l.

Option B) ls -l is the correct choice for listing files and directories in a long listing format in Linux. When you execute this command, it displays detailed information about each file and directory in the specified location. Here's a breakdown of what each part of the command does:

"ls" is the command used to list files and directories.

"-l" is an option used with the "ls" command to generate a long listing format. This format displays information such as file permissions, ownership, size, and modification time for each file and directory.

Let's briefly discuss the other options:

ls -a: This command lists all files and directories, including hidden ones, but it does not provide detailed information in a long listing format.

ls -h: This option is used to display file sizes in a human-readable format, such as kilobytes (K), megabytes (M), etc. It does not produce a long listing format.

ls -R: This option is used to recursively list all files and directories in the specified location and its subdirectories. It does not generate a long listing format.

Therefore, option B) ls -l is the correct choice for listing files and directories in a detailed long listing format in Linux.

Question 39:

What is the effect of the command cp -r directory1 directory2 in Linux?

A) Copies directory1 into directory2

B) Copies the contents of directory1 into directory2

(Correct)

C) Moves directory1 into directory2

D) Deletes directory1

Explanation

The correct answer is B) Copies the contents of directory1 into directory2.

Option B) accurately describes the effect of the command cp -r directory1 directory2. Let's break down the command and its functionality:

cp: This is the command used to copy files and directories in Linux.

-r: This option stands for "recursive" and is used to copy directories and their contents recursively.

directory1: This is the source directory that contains the files and subdirectories to be copied.

directory2: This is the destination directory where the contents of directory1 will be copied.

When you execute cp -r directory1 directory2, the command copies all files and subdirectories from directory1 into directory2, preserving their structure. However, it does not copy the directory1 itself; instead, it copies its contents.

Let's briefly discuss the other options:

Copies directory1 into directory2: This option is incorrect because the cp command with the -r option does not copy the entire directory1 itself; it copies its contents into directory2.

Moves directory1 into directory2: This option is incorrect because the cp command with the -r option copies the contents of directory1 into directory2; it does not move directory1.

Deletes directory1: This option is incorrect because the cp command does not delete directory1. It only copies its contents into another directory.

Therefore, option B) accurately represents the effect of the command cp -r directory1 directory2, which is to copy the contents of directory1 into directory2.

Question 40:

Which wildcard character in Linux represents zero, one, or

more occurrences of any character?

A) ?

B) *

(Correct)

C) []

D) {}

Explanation

The correct answer is B) *.

Option B) * represents the wildcard character in Linux that matches zero, one, or more occurrences of any character. Let's delve into the Explanation:

(asterisk): This wildcard character matches any sequence of characters, including zero characters. It's commonly used for pattern matching in Linux commands such as ls, cp, mv, rm, etc. For example, ls *.txt will list all files ending with .txt in the current directory.

Now, let's briefly discuss the other options:

? (Question mark): This wildcard character matches exactly one occurrence of any character. For instance, ls file?.txt will match files like file1.txt, fileA.txt, but not file12.txt.

[] (square brackets): This wildcard character matches any single character within the specified range or set. For example, ls file[123].txt will match files like file1.txt, file2.txt, or file3.txt.

{} (curly braces): This is not a wildcard character, but rather a brace expansion feature in Linux. It allows for generating arbitrary strings or sequences. For example, cp file{1,2}.txt will copy file1.txt and file2.txt to the destination.

Therefore, option B) * is the correct choice as it represents the wildcard character in Linux that matches zero, one, or more occurrences of any character.

Question 41:

What is the effect of the command rm -rf directory in Linux?

A) Removes the directory forcefully without confirmation

B) Removes the directory and its contents recursively without confirmation

(Correct)

C) Removes the directory only if it's empty

D) Renames the directory

Explanation

The correct answer is B) Removes the directory and its contents recursively without confirmation.

Option B) accurately describes the effect of the command rm -rf directory. Let's break down the command and its functionality:

rm: This is the command used to remove files and directories in Linux.

-rf: These are options used with the rm command:

-r stands for "recursive," which allows the removal of directories and their contents recursively.

-f stands for "force," which removes files forcefully without asking for confirmation.

When you execute rm -rf directory, the command removes the specified directory and all its contents, including subdirectories and files, without prompting for confirmation. This command is commonly used for deleting directories and their contents in one go.

Let's briefly discuss the other options:

Removes the directory forcefully without confirmation: This option is partially correct. While it mentions removing the directory forcefully, it doesn't emphasize that it also removes its contents recursively.

Removes the directory only if it's empty: This option is incorrect because the -r option with rm allows the removal of non-empty directories and their contents.

Renames the directory: This option is incorrect because the rm command is used for removal, not renaming.

Therefore, option B) accurately represents the effect of the command rm -rf directory, which is to remove the directory and its contents recursively without confirmation.

Question 42:

Which command is used to create a new, empty file in Linux?

A) touch

(Correct)

B) cp

C) mkdir

D) mv

Explanation

The correct answer is A) touch.

Option A) touch is the command used to create a new, empty file in Linux. Let's delve into the Explanation:

touch: This command is used to create empty files or update the access and modification timestamps of existing files. When used with a filename that doesn't exist, it creates a new empty file with that name.

Now, let's briefly discuss the other options:

B) cp: This command is used to copy files and directories, not to create empty files.

mkdir: This command is used to create directories, not empty files.

mv: This command is used to move or rename files and directories, not to create empty files.

Therefore, option A) touch is the correct choice as it represents the command used to create a new, empty file in Linux.

Question 43:

What is the numerical file descriptor assigned to the standard error channel (stderr) in Linux?

A) 0

B) 1

(Correct)

C) 2

D) 3

Explanation

In Linux, the numerical file descriptor assigned to the standard error channel (stderr) is 2.

Question 44:

Which symbol is used to redirect the standard output of a process to a file in Linux?

A) <

B) >

(Correct)

C) |

D) &

Explanation

The greater than symbol (>) is used to redirect the standard output of a process to a file in Linux.

Question 45:

How would you redirect both the standard output and standard error of a process to a file named "output.txt"?

A) > output.txt 2>

B) &> output.txt

(Correct)

C) 2> output.txt 1>

D) > output.txt 1&>

Explanation

The "&>" operator is used to redirect both stdout and stderr to a file in Linux.

Question 46:

Which command is used to display how many times a repeated line appears in a text in Linux?

A) cat

B) set

C) uniq

(Correct)

D) wc

Explanation

The "uniq" command in Linux is used to display how many times a repeated line appears in a text.

Question 47:

What is the purpose of the tee command in Linux?

A) To count the number of lines, words, and characters in a text

B) To display the contents of a file

C) To create a one-way communication channel between two processes

D) To display output on the screen and store it in a file simultaneously

(Correct)

Explanation

The "tee" command in Linux is used to display output on the

screen and store it in a file simultaneously.

Question 48:

What command is used to display active jobs and their status in a Linux system?

A) ps

B) top

C) jobs

(Correct)

D) watch

Explanation

The `jobs` command is used to display active jobs and their status, particularly those that have been sent to the background or suspended.

Question 49:

Which utility is used to bring a job to the foreground in a Linux terminal?

A) fg

(Correct)

B) bg

C) kill

D) nohup

Explanation

The `fg` command is used to bring a job to the foreground in a

Linux terminal, allowing the user to interact with it directly.

Question 50:

What does the plus sign (+) indicate in the output of the `jobs` command?

A) Currently running job

B) Previously suspended job

C) Default job

(Correct)

D) Terminated job

Explanation

The plus sign (+) indicates the default job, which is the last job that was suspended or sent to the background.

Question 51:

Which command is used to detach a job from the current session in Linux?

A) fg

B) bg

C) nohup

(Correct)

D) kill

Explanation

The `nohup` command is used to detach a job from the current session, allowing it to continue running even after the session is closed.

Question 52:

What signal is sent by default when using the `kill` command without specifying a signal?

A) SIGKILL

B) SIGSTOP

C) SIGTERM

(Correct)

D) SIGINT

Explanation

The `kill` command sends a SIGTERM signal by default, which allows the process to gracefully terminate.

Question 53:

Which command is used to monitor CPU and memory usage dynamically in Linux?

A) top

(Correct)

B) ps

C) watch

D) free

Explanation

The `top` command is used to monitor CPU and memory usage dynamically, providing real-time updates.

Question 54:

What option is used with the `watch` command to specify the update interval?

A) -i

B) -u

C) -n

(Correct)

D) -t

Explanation

The `-n` option is used with the `watch` command to specify the update interval in seconds.

Question 55:

What term is used to describe operating systems capable of running more than one process at the same time?

A) Multi-threading systems

B) Single-tasking systems

C) Multi-processing systems

(Correct)

D) Sequential systems

Explanation

Multi-processing systems can run multiple processes simultaneously, either through true simultaneity with multiple processing units or by quickly switching between processes on a single processor.

Question 56:

In Linux, which file provides information about the static priority of a running process?

A) /etc/process_priority

B) /proc/sched

C) /proc/[PID]/sched

(Correct)

D) /etc/scheduler

Explanation

The static priority of a running process can be found in the sched file located in its respective directory inside the /proc filesystem, using the path /proc/[PID]/sched.

Question 57:

What is the default priority value for normal processes in Linux?

A) 0

B) 50

C) 100

D) 120

(Correct)

Explanation

Normal processes in Linux have a default priority value of 120, which can be adjusted using the nice command.

Question 58:

What is the purpose of the `grep` command in Linux?

A) To search for files in a directory

B) To display the contents of a file

C) To find and replace text in files

D) To search for patterns in text files

(Correct)

Explanation

The `grep` command is used to search for patterns or regular expressions in text files.

Question 59:

Which option is used with the `grep` command to count the total number of lines with matches?

A) -i

B) -c

(Correct)

C) -v

D) -n

Explanation

The `-c` option with the `grep` command is used to count the total number of lines with matches.

Question 60:

What is the purpose of the `sed` command in Linux?

A) To search for patterns in text files

B) To edit text files interactively

C) To manipulate text based on predefined instructions

(Correct)

D) To display the contents of a file

Explanation

The `sed` command is a stream editor used to manipulate text based on predefined instructions or scripts.

Question 61:

Which `sed` command is used to delete the first line of a text stream?

A) d

(Correct)

B) c

C) a

D) s

Explanation

The `d` command in `sed` is used to delete lines.

Question 62:

Which of the following modes does the vi editor provide?

A) Normal mode and Visual mode

B) Insert mode and Replace mode

C) Command mode and Insert mode

(Correct)

D) Navigation mode and Editing mode

Explanation

The vi editor provides different modes of operation, including Command mode (also known as Normal mode) and Insert mode. In Command mode, users can navigate and perform editing tasks using keyboard commands, while in Insert mode, users can input text directly into the document.

Question 63:

What is the purpose of the `vimtutor` command in Linux?

A) To launch the Vim editor with a tutorial file.

B) To provide a step-by-step guide for using the vi editor.

(Correct)

C) To open a tutorial for the nano text editor.

D) To initiate a guided tour of the Emacs editor.

Explanation

The `vimtutor` command opens a tutorial for the vi editor (or its improved version, vim) in Linux. It offers users a step-by-step guide to learn and practice vi editor commands.

Question 64:

Which command in vi allows you to undo the last action?

A) u

(Correct)

B) Ctrl-R

C) :undo

D) Esc

Explanation

In vi, pressing the `u` key in Normal mode allows you to undo the last action performed, reverting the document to its previous state.

Question 65:

Which command is commonly used to manage MBR partitions on Linux systems?

A) gdisk

B) mkfs

C) fdisk

(Correct)

D) parted

Explanation

fdisk is the standard utility for managing MBR partitions on Linux systems.

Question 66:

What is the primary limitation of the MBR partitioning scheme?

A) Limited to 4 primary partitions per disk

(Correct)

B) Inability to address disks of more than 2 TB in size

C) Lack of support for GUID Partition Table (GPT)

D) Incompatibility with modern operating systems

Explanation

MBR has a limitation of only 4 primary partitions per disk.

Question 67:

Which partitioning system addresses many of the limitations of MBR, including support for larger disk sizes and more partitions?

A) NTFS

B) FAT32

C) GPT

(Correct)

D) ext4

Explanation

GUID Partition Table (GPT) addresses many limitations of MBR, such as disk size and partition count restrictions.

Question 68:

What command is used to print the current partition table in the gdisk utility?

A) p

(Correct)

B) print

C) list

D) info

Explanation

In gdisk, the command "p" is used to print the current partition table.

Question 69:

Which filesystem is commonly used for servers and environments requiring high performance and reliability?

A) NTFS

B) FAT32

C) ext4

D) XFS

(Correct)

Explanation

XFS is a high-performance filesystem commonly used for servers and environments requiring high performance and reliability.

Question 70:

What command is used to display the amount of disk space used by directories and files recursively?

A) df

B) fsck

C) du

(Correct)

D) xfs_repair

Explanation

The `du` command is used to display disk usage of files and directories recursively.

Question 71:

Which parameter of the `du` command displays output in a more human-readable format, such as KB, MB, or GB?

A) -k

B) -h

(Correct)

C) -r

D) -s

Explanation

The `-h` parameter of the `du` command stands for "human-readable" and formats the output accordingly.

Question 72:

Which command is used to display information about available disk space and filesystems?

A) df

(Correct)

B) fsck

C) du

D) xfs_repair

Explanation

The `df` command is used to display information about disk space usage and available filesystems.

Question 73:

Which parameter of the `df` command displays output in a human-readable format?

A) -k

B) -h

(Correct)

C) -r

D) -s

Explanation

The `-h` parameter of the `df` command formats output in a human-readable format.

Question 74:

What command is used to manually mount a filesystem in Linux?

A) mountpoint

B) mountfs

C) mount

(Correct)

D) filesystem

Explanation

The `mount` command is used to manually mount a filesystem in Linux. It attaches the filesystem to a specific point in the system's directory tree, known as the mount point.

Question 75:

Which parameter is used with the `mount` command to specify the type of filesystem being mounted?

A) -d

B) -t

(Correct)

C) -f

D) -m

Explanation

The `-t` parameter in the `mount` command is used to specify the type of filesystem being mounted, for example, ext4, exFAT, NTFS, etc.

Question 76:

What is the purpose of the `/etc/fstab` file in Linux?

A) To store system configuration settings

B) To list all mounted filesystems

C) To specify the filesystems that can be mounted during bootup

(Correct)

D) To track filesystem usage

Explanation

The `/etc/fstab` file contains descriptions about the filesystems that can be mounted, including their mount points, types, and mount options. It is used during system bootup to mount filesystems automatically.

Question 77:

How can you force the unmounting of a filesystem in Linux?

A) Using the `-f` parameter with the `umount` command

(Correct)

B) Using the `-r` parameter with the `umount` command

C) Using the `-x` parameter with the `umount` command

D) Using the `-u` parameter with the `umount` command

Explanation

The `-f` parameter with the `umount` command is used to

force the unmounting of a filesystem, even if it is busy.

Question 78:

Which command is used to obtain a detailed listing of files, including permissions, ownership, and other attributes?

A) dir

B) ls -l

(Correct)

C) ls -a

D) list

Explanation

The `ls -l` command provides a detailed listing of files, including permissions, ownership, file size, and modification date.

Question 79:

What does the command `chmod 755 file.txt` do?

A) Grants read and execute permissions to the owner, and read-only permissions to the group and others.

B) Grants read, write, and execute permissions to the owner, and read and execute permissions to the group and others.

C) Grants full permissions (read, write, and execute) to the owner, and read and execute permissions to the group and others.

(Correct)

D) Grants execute permissions to the owner, group, and others, and read-only permissions to the owner.

Explanation

In octal notation, 7 corresponds to read, write, and execute permissions, while 5 corresponds to read and execute permissions.

Question 80:

What is the primary difference between a symbolic link and a hard link in Linux?

A) Symbolic links point to a file's inode, while hard links create duplicate inodes.

B) Symbolic links can traverse partitions and filesystems, while hard links cannot.

C) Hard links preserve the original file's inode, while symbolic links create a new inode.

(Correct)

D) Hard links are created with the `ln` command, while symbolic links are created with the `ls` command.

Explanation

Hard links create additional directory entries pointing to the same inode as the original file, while symbolic links create a new inode that points to the target file's path.

Question 81:

Which command is used to create a symbolic link in Linux?

A) mv

B) cp

C) ln -s

(Correct)

D) touch

Explanation

The `-s` option is used with the `ln` command to create symbolic links.

Question 82:

What happens if you delete the target file of a symbolic link in Linux?

A) The symbolic link becomes invalid.

B) The symbolic link becomes a hard link.

C) The symbolic link is automatically updated to point to the next available file.

D) The symbolic link remains intact but points to a non-existent file.

(Correct)

Explanation

Symbolic links continue to exist even if the target file is deleted, but they point to a non-existent file in this case.

Question 83:

How can you identify a symbolic link when listing files in a directory in Linux?

A) Symbolic links have a 'l' as the first character in the permissions field.

(Correct)

B) Symbolic links have an 's' as the first character in the permissions field.

C) Symbolic links are displayed in a different color compared to regular files.

D) Symbolic links are listed after all regular files in the directory listing.

Explanation

When using the `ls -l` command, symbolic links are indicated by an 'l' as the first character in the permissions field.

Question 84:

What is the purpose of the Filesystem Hierarchy Standard (FHS) on Linux systems?

A) To enforce mandatory compliance with directory structures.

B) To provide a standardized layout for the filesystem.

(Correct)

C) To restrict the access of users to specific directories.

D) To define the format of filesystems used in Linux.

Explanation

The FHS defines a standard directory structure for Linux systems, facilitating interoperability and system administration.

Question 85:

Which directory contains essential binaries available to all users?

A) /usr

B) /bin

(Correct)

C) /lib

D) /etc

Explanation

The /bin directory contains essential binaries that are fundamental to the operation of the system and are available to all users.

Question 86:

Where would you typically find user-mountable removable media on a Linux system?

A) /mnt

B) /dev

C) /media

(Correct)

D) /var

Explanation

User-mountable removable media, such as flash drives and external disks, are typically mounted under the /media directory.

Question 87:

Which directory contains data served by the system, such as web pages?

A) /opt

B) /srv

(Correct)

C) /run

D) /var

Explanation

The /srv directory contains data served by the system, such as web pages served by a web server.

Question 88:

What is the purpose of the /tmp directory according to the FHS?

A) To store temporary files that persist between reboots.

B) To store runtime variable data used by running processes.

C) To provide a mount point for temporarily mounted filesystems.

D) To store temporary files that are erased during system boot-up.

(Correct)

Explanation

According to the FHS, the /tmp directory is used to store temporary files that are erased during system boot-up.

Question 89:

Which command is used to search for files and directories based on various criteria on a Linux system?

A) locate

B) updatedb

C) find

(Correct)

D) whereis

Explanation

The find command is used to search for files and directories based on various criteria, such as name, size, and permissions.

Question 90:

What is the purpose of the updatedb command in Linux?

A) To update the Linux kernel.

B) To update the system's package database.

C) To update the locate command's database of files.

(Correct)

D) To update the system's configuration files.

Explanation

The updatedb command updates the database used by the locate command to quickly search for files.

PRACTICE TEST TWO - LPIC-1 EXAM 101 VERSION: 5.0

90 questions | 2 hours | 90% correct required to pass

The LPIC-1 Exam 101 Version: 5.0 Practice Test is a comprehensive resource designed to prepare you for the LPIC-1 (Linux Professional Institute Certification) Exam 101. It includes practice questions that mimic the format and content of the actual test. Each **Question** comes with a detailed **Explanation** to help you understand the concepts better. This practice test is an excellent tool to harness the power of Linux and achieve LPIC-1 certification.

Note

The 101 actual exam is a 90-minute exam with 60 multiple-choice and fill-in-the-blank questions.

Question 1:

What command is used to list all currently loaded kernel modules in a Linux system?

A) lsusb

B) lspci

C) lsmod

(Correct)

D) modprobe

Explanation

The lsmod command is used to list all currently loaded kernel modules in a Linux system.

Question 2:

Which command is used to load and unload kernel modules in a running Linux system?

A) modinfo

B) lsmod

C) modprobe

(Correct)

D) insmod

Explanation

The modprobe command is used to load and unload kernel modules in a running Linux system.

Question 3:

What is the purpose of the `initramfs` in the Linux boot process?

A) Execute system initialization scripts

B) Load the kernel into RAM

C) Provide required modules for accessing the root filesystem

(Correct)

D) Manage hardware resources

Explanation

The `initramfs` (initial RAM filesystem) provides the required modules so that the kernel can access the root filesystem of the operating system.

Question 4:

Which systemd feature allows service activation via sockets and D-Bus?

A) cgroups

B) On-demand daemon execution

(Correct)

C) Dependency-based service control

D) System session recovery

Explanation

On-demand daemon execution in systemd allows service activation via sockets and D-Bus, improving system efficiency.

Question 5:

Which command is used to inspect kernel ring buffer messages in a Linux system?

A) klog

B) bootlog

C) dmesg

(Correct)

D) kernellog

Explanation

The `dmesg` command is used to display kernel ring buffer messages, including boot messages.

Question 6:

Which directory contains initialization logs in a Linux system based on systemd?

A) /var/log/journal/

(Correct)

B) /var/log/init/

C) /var/log/syslog/

D) /var/log/boot/

Explanation

In systemd-based systems, initialization logs are stored in the directory /var/log/journal/.

Question 7:

Which command is used to put the system in low power mode in systemd?

A) systemctl shutdown

B) systemctl suspend

(Correct)

C) systemctl poweroff

D) systemctl hibernate

Explanation

The systemctl suspend command is used to put the system in low power mode in systemd.

Question 8:

Where are the configuration files associated with systemd units located?

A) /etc/init.d/

B) /etc/systemd/

C) /lib/systemd/system/

(Correct)

D) /etc/rc.d/

Explanation

The configuration files associated with systemd units are located in the /lib/systemd/system/ directory.

Question 9:

Which command is used to list all available systemd units and show if they are enabled to start when the system boots?

A) systemctl list-units

B) systemctl list-unit-files

(Correct)

C) systemctl show-units

D) systemctl display-units

Explanation

The systemctl list-unit-files command lists all available systemd units and shows if they are enabled to start when the system boots.

Question 10:

In a SysVinit system, which command is used to send a message to terminal sessions of all logged-in users?

A) wall

(Correct)

B) write

C) talk

D) msg

Explanation

The wall command is used to send a message to terminal sessions of all logged-in users in a SysVinit system.

Question 11:

Which utility is used to format a swap partition in Linux?

A) mkfs

B) mkswap

(Correct)

C) fsck

D) swapon

Explanation

The mkswap utility is used to set up a swap partition in Linux.

Question 12:

What is the primary benefit of Logical Volume Management (LVM) in Linux?

A) It simplifies disk partitioning.

B) It improves filesystem performance.

C) It provides better security for data.

D) It offers more flexible management of disk space.

(Correct)

Explanation

Logical Volume Management (LVM) provides a more flexible approach to managing disk space than traditional partitioning methods.

Question 13:

Which directory is traditionally used as the mount point for external devices in Linux?

A) /mnt

(Correct)

B) /var

C) /media

D) /home

Explanation

The /mnt directory is traditionally used as the mount point for external devices in Linux.

Question 14:

What is the purpose of the /boot partition in Linux?

A) To store system logs.

B) To contain bootloader-related files.

(Correct)

C) To hold user home directories.

D) To manage swap space.

Explanation

The /boot partition in Linux contains files used by the bootloader to load the operating system.

Question 15:

What is the purpose of the /boot partition on Linux systems?

A) To store user data.

B) To mount the root file system.

C) To separate boot-related files from the rest of the filesystem.

(Correct)

D) To allocate memory for system processes.

Explanation

The /boot partition on Linux systems is used to store boot-related files, separating them from the root file system.

Question 16:

How can GRUB 2 be installed on a system?

A) Using the update-grub utility.

B) Using the fdisk command.

C) Using the grub-install utility.

(Correct)

D) Using the mkfs command.

Explanation

GRUB 2 can be installed on a system using the grub-install utility.

Question 17:

Which file contains the default configuration for GRUB 2?

A) /etc/grub.conf

B) /boot/grub/menu.lst

C) /etc/default/grub

D) /boot/grub/grub.cfg

(Correct)

Explanation

The default configuration file for GRUB 2 is /boot/grub/grub.cfg.

Question 18:

What command is used to update the GRUB configuration file in GRUB 2?

A) grub-update

B) grub-config

C) grub-mkconfig

(Correct)

D) update-grub

(Correct)

Explanation

The command used to update the GRUB configuration file in GRUB 2 is update-grub or grub-mkconfig.

Question 19:

How are static libraries different from shared libraries?

A) Static libraries are linked dynamically at run time.

B) Static libraries embed library code into the program at link time.

(Correct)

C) Shared libraries increase program size.

D) Shared libraries are not reusable.

Explanation

The correct answer is B) Static libraries embed library code into the program at link time, while shared libraries are dynamically linked at run time.

Question 20:

Which directory typically contains configuration files for shared library paths in a Linux system?

A) /etc/bin

B) /usr/bin

C) /etc/ld.so.conf.d

(Correct)

D) /lib64

Explanation

The correct answer is C) Configuration files for shared library paths are typically found in the directory /etc/ld.so.conf.d.

Question 21:

What command is used to update the cache file of shared library paths in a Linux system?

A) `ldconfig`

(Correct)

B) `ldd`

C) `ls`

D) `ldupdate`

Explanation

The correct answer is A) The `ldconfig` command updates the

cache file of shared library paths in a Linux system.

Question 22:

Which command is used to update the package index before installing or upgrading software packages with APT?

A) apt-get update

(Correct)

B) apt-get install

C) apt-get upgrade

D) apt-get remove

Explanation

The "update" parameter is used with apt-get to update the package index.

Question 23:

What is the purpose of the "purge" parameter in dpkg?

A) To remove a package and its configuration files

(Correct)

B) To force installation of a package

C) To list the contents of a package

D) To reconfigure an installed package

Explanation

The "purge" parameter is used with dpkg to remove a package and its configuration files from the system.

Question 24:

Which command is used to remove a package with APT, including its configuration files?

A) apt-get remove

B) apt-get purge

(Correct)

C) apt-get clean

D) apt-get autoremove

Explanation

The "purge" parameter is used with apt-get to remove a package and its configuration files.

Question 25:

How do you install a package with `yum`?

A) `yum add PACKAGENAME`

B) `yum install PACKAGENAME`

(Correct)

C) `yum upgrade PACKAGENAME`

D) `yum update PACKAGENAME`

Explanation

The `install` option with `yum` is used to install a package.

Question 26:

Which command is used to search for packages with `yum`?

A) `yum search PATTERN`

(Correct)

B) `yum find PATTERN`

C) `yum locate PATTERN`

D) `yum query PATTERN`

Explanation

The `search` option with `yum` is used to search for packages by name or description.

Question 27:

What does the `dnf` command stand for?

A) Dandified YUM

(Correct)

B) Debian Network Framework

C) Dependency Network Finder

D) Dynamic Network Facility

Explanation

`dnf` stands for Dandified YUM, and it is a fork of YUM used for package management on Fedora systems.

Question 28:

Which command is used to list installed packages with `dnf`?

A) `dnf list-installed`

(Correct)

B) `dnf show-installed`

C) `dnf installed`

D) `dnf info-installed`

Explanation

The `list-installed` option with `dnf` is used to list installed packages.

Question 29:

Which disk image type allows for dynamic allocation of disk space?

A) RAW

B) Sparse

C) COW

(Correct)

D) Pre-allocated

Explanation

C) Copy-on-write (COW) disk images allow for dynamic allocation of disk space as new data is written to the disk.

Question 30:

What utility is used to pre-configure Linux systems deployed in the cloud?

A) systemd-nspawn

B) Docker

C) cloud-init

(Correct)

D) OpenShift

Explanation

C) cloud-init is a utility used to pre-configure Linux systems deployed in the cloud by applying settings from YAML configuration files during initial boot-up.

Question 31:

How can an administrator securely access a remote virtual guest on a cloud platform?

A) Through FTP protocol

B) Using Telnet

C) Via SSH

(Correct)

D) By accessing a web-based console

Explanation

C) The most prevalent method for accessing a remote virtual guest on a cloud platform is through SSH (Secure Shell).

Question 32:

Which command is used to create a new environment variable in Linux?

A) `set`

B) `addenv`

C) `createenv`

D) `export`

(Correct)

Explanation

The correct answer is D) `export`. You can create a new environment variable using the `export` command followed by the variable name and value.

Question 33:

How can you check the value of an environment variable named `myvar` in Linux?

A) `printenv myvar`

B) `echo myvar`

(Correct)

C) `env myvar`

D) `checkenv myvar`

Explanation

The correct answer is B) `echo myvar`. Using `echo` followed by the variable name (preceded by `$`) will print its value.

Question 34:

What command is used to unset or delete an environment variable in Linux?

A) `remove`

B) `unset`

(Correct)

C) `deleteenv`

D) `clear`

Explanation

The correct answer is B) `unset`. The `unset` command is used to remove or unset an environment variable.

Question 35:

What does the `od` command do in Linux?

A) Counts the number of words in a file.

B) Displays a file's contents in octal format.

(Correct)

C) Removes duplicate lines from a file.

D) Displays the first 10 lines of a file.

Explanation

The correct answer is B) The `od` command displays a file's contents in octal format.

Question 36:

How can you verify the integrity of a file using its checksum value in Linux?

A) Using the `cat` command.

B) Using the `ls` command.

C) Using the `sha256sum` command.

(Correct)

D) Using the `grep` command.

Explanation

The correct answer is C) The `sha256sum` command is used to calculate and verify the checksum value of a file.

Question 37:

How do you list all files in the current directory, including hidden files, in Linux?

A) ls -a

(Correct)

B) ls -l

C) ls -h

D) ls -R

Explanation

The correct answer is A) ls -a.

Option A) ls -a is the command used to list all files in the current directory, including hidden files, in Linux. Let's break down the command and its functionality:

ls: This is the command used to list files and directories in Linux.

-a: This option stands for "all" and directs the ls command to show all files, including hidden files. Hidden files in Linux are those whose filenames begin with a dot (.), and they are typically configuration files or directories.

Now, let's briefly discuss the other options:

B) ls -l: This command lists files and directories in the long listing format, showing detailed information such as file permissions, ownership, size, and modification time, but it does not include hidden files unless combined with the -a option.

C) ls -h: This option is used to display file sizes in a human-readable format, such as kilobytes (K), megabytes (M), etc. It does not include hidden files.

D) ls -R: This option is used to recursively list all files and directories in the current directory and its subdirectories, but it does not specifically include hidden files unless combined with the -a option.

Therefore, option A) ls -a is the correct choice as it represents the command used to list all files in the current directory, including hidden files, in Linux.

Question 38:

Which command is used to search for files in Linux based on their modification time?

A) find -size

B) find -name

C) find -mtime

(Correct)

D) find -type

Explanation

The correct answer is C) find -mtime.

Option C) find -mtime is the command used to search for files in Linux based on their modification time. Let's delve into the explanation:

find: This is the command used to search for files and directories within a specified directory hierarchy in Linux.

-mtime: This option is used with the find command to specify the modification time of files. It allows you to search for files based on the number of days since their content was last modified. For example, -mtime +1 will find files modified more than one day ago, while -mtime -1 will find files modified less than one day ago.

Now, let's briefly discuss the other options:

find -size: This option is used to search for files based on their size, not their modification time.

find -name: This option is used to search for files based on their filenames, not their modification time.

find -type: This option is used to search for files based on their type (e.g., regular file, directory, symbolic link), not their modification time.

Therefore, option C) find -mtime is the correct choice as it represents the command used to search for files in Linux based on their modification time.

Question 39:

What is the effect of the command tar -cvf archive.tar directory in Linux?

A) Creates a compressed archive of the directory

B) Creates a tar archive of the directory

(Correct)

C) Extracts the contents of the archive into the directory

D) Deletes the directory

Explanation

The correct answer is B) Creates a tar archive of the directory.

Option B) accurately describes the effect of the command tar -cvf archive.tar directory. Let's break down the command and its functionality:

tar: This is the command used in Linux for archiving files and directories.

-c: This option stands for "create" and directs the tar command to create a new archive.

-v: This option stands for "verbose" and instructs tar to display the files being archived.

-f archive.tar: This option specifies the name of the archive file to be created.

directory: This is the directory or directories to be included in the archive.

When you execute tar -cvf archive.tar directory, the command creates a new tar archive named archive.tar containing the contents of the specified directory.

Now, let's briefly discuss the other options:

Creates a compressed archive of the directory: This option is incorrect because the -c option with tar creates a tar archive, but it does not compress the archive. To create a compressed archive, you would typically use additional tools like gzip or bzip2, or specify compression options with tar.

Extracts the contents of the archive into the directory: This option is incorrect because the -c option with tar is used to create an archive, not extract files from an existing archive. To extract files, you would use the -x option with tar.

Deletes the directory: This option is incorrect because the tar command is used for archiving files, not for deleting directories.

Therefore, option B) accurately represents the effect of the command tar -cvf archive.tar directory, which is to create a tar archive of the specified directory.

Question 40:

Which command is used to extract the contents of a tar archive in Linux?

A) tar -cvf

B) tar -xvf

(Correct)

C) tar -zxf

D) tar -rf

Explanation

The correct answer is B) tar -xvf.

Option B) tar -xvf is the command used to extract the contents of a tar archive in Linux. Let's delve into the explanation:

tar: This is the command used in Linux for archiving and extracting files.

-x: This option stands for "extract" and directs the tar command to extract files from the archive.

-v: This option stands for "verbose" and instructs tar to display the files being extracted.

-f: This option specifies the name of the archive file from which to extract files.

When you execute tar -xvf archive.tar, the command extracts the contents of the tar archive archive.tar into the current directory.

Now, let's briefly discuss the other options:

tar -cvf: This option is used to create a new tar archive. The -c option stands for "create."

tar -zxf: This option is used to extract files from a compressed tar archive (also known as a "tarball") that has been compressed using gzip (*.tar.gz or *.tgz). The -z option is used to specify gzip compression.

tar -rf: This option is used to add or update files or directories to an existing tar archive. The -r option stands for "append."

Therefore, option B) tar -xvf is the correct choice as it represents the command used to extract the contents of a tar archive in Linux.

Question 41:

What is the purpose of the find command in Linux?

A) To create new files

B) To search for files and directories based on various criteria

(Correct)

C) To copy files and directories

D) To delete files and directories

Explanation

The correct answer is B) To search for files and directories based on various criteria.

Option B) accurately describes the purpose of the find command in Linux. Let's delve into the explanation:

The find command in Linux is used to search for files and directories within a specified directory hierarchy based on various criteria such as filename, permissions, modification time, size, type, and more. It provides a powerful and flexible way to locate files and directories that match specific patterns or attributes.

Here's how the find command typically works:

$ find [starting_directory] [options] [criteria]

[starting_directory]: This is the directory where the search begins. If not specified, the search starts from the current directory.

[options]: These are various options that modify the behavior of the find command, such as specifying the type of files to search for (-type), controlling the depth of the search (-maxdepth, -mindepth), and more.

[criteria]: These are the conditions or criteria used to filter the search results, such as filename patterns, permissions, modification time, size, etc.

For example, to find all files named example.txt within the current directory and its subdirectories, you would use the following command:

$ find . -name "example.txt"

Now, let's briefly discuss the other options:

To create new files: This option is incorrect. The find command is used for searching files and directories, not for creating new files.

To copy files and directories: This option is incorrect. The find command is primarily used for searching files and directories, although it can be combined with other commands like cp for copying files found by find.

To delete files and directories: This option is incorrect. The find command does not delete files and directories directly. However, it can be combined with the rm command to delete files that match certain criteria.

Therefore, option B) accurately represents the purpose of the find command in Linux, which is to search for files and directories based on various criteria.

Question 42:

Which symbol is used to create a pipeline connecting the output of one program to the input of another program in Linux?

A) <

B) >

C) |

(Correct)

D) &

Explanation

The pipe symbol (|) is used to create a pipeline connecting the output of one program to the input of another program in Linux.

Question 43:

What does command substitution allow in Linux?

A) To redirect the output of a command to a file

B) To replace a command with its standard input

C) To store the output of a command in a variable or use it as an argument to another command

(Correct)

D) To concatenate multiple files into one

Explanation

Command substitution in Linux allows to store the output of a command in a variable or use it as an argument to another command.

Question 44:

Which program is used to run a given command with arguments provided by another program's output in Linux?

A) cat

B) grep

C) xargs

(Correct)

D) sort

Explanation

The "xargs" program in Linux is used to run a given command with arguments provided by another program's output.

Question 45:

In Linux, what is the purpose of the find command with the -exec option?

A) To search for files and directories based on specified criteria

B) To execute a command for each search result item

(Correct)

C) To print the contents of files

D) To create symbolic links between files

Explanation

In Linux, the find command with the -exec option is used to execute a command for each search result item.

Question 46:

Which option should be used with the xargs command to limit how many lines will be used as arguments per command execution in Linux?

A) -n

B) -L

(Correct)

C) -i

D) -a

Explanation

The "-L" option is used with the xargs command in Linux to limit how many lines will be used as arguments per command execution.

Question 47:

Which command is used to kill processes based on their name in Linux?

A) pkill

(Correct)

B) killall

C) pgrep

D) kill

Explanation

The `pkill` command is used to kill processes based on their name, allowing for more convenient termination.

Question 48:

What does the STAT column in the output of `ps` command represent?

A) Process ID

B) Priority of process

C) Status of process

(Correct)

D) Percentage of CPU usage

Explanation

The STAT column in the output of the `ps` command represents the status of the process, such as whether it is running, sleeping, or stopped.

Question 49:

How can you change the priority of a process using the `top` command?

A) Press P and enter the new priority value

B) Press k and enter the PID of the process

C) Press r and enter the new priority value

(Correct)

D) Press u and specify the username

Explanation

You can change the priority of a process in `top` by pressing r and entering the new priority value when prompted.

Question 50:

Which command is used to list processes started by a specific user?

A) ps -u

(Correct)

B) top -u

C) ps --user

D) top --user

Explanation

The `ps -u` command is used to list processes started by a specific user in Linux.

Question 51:

What does the TASKS row in the summary area of `top` command output represent?

A) Total number of processes

(Correct)

B) Total number of users logged in

C) Total CPU usage percentage

D) Total memory usage percentage

Explanation

The TASKS row in the summary area of `top` command output represents the total number of processes, including those running, sleeping, stopped, or in zombie state.

Question 52:

oneko is a delightful program that displays a cat chasing your mouse cursor. If not already installed in your desktop system, install it using your distribution's package manager. We will use it to study job control. Start the program in background. How do you do that?

A) oneko &

B) oneko

C) oneko | bg

D) oneko | &

Move the mouse cursor to see how the cat chases it. Now suspend the process. How do you do that? What is the output?

A) Press Ctrl + Z. Output: Suspended

B) Press Ctrl + C. Output: Program exits.

C) Type stop oneko. Output: Program is stopped.

D) Type pause oneko. Output: Program is paused.

Check how many jobs you currently have. What do you type? What is the output?

A) jobs. Output: Displays list of jobs.

B) list. Output: Displays list of jobs.

C) check. Output: No such command.

D) ps. Output: Displays all processes.

Now send it to the background specifying its job ID. What is the output? How can you tell the job is running in the background?

A) bg %1. Output: Job ID and message confirming job is running in the background.

B) background %1. Output: No such command.

C) bg oneko. Output: Job ID and message confirming job is running in the background.

D) runbg %1. Output: No such command.

Finally, terminate the job specifying its job ID. What do you type?

A) kill %1

B) terminate %1

C) end %1

D) stop %1

1. C), A), B), A), A)

(Correct)

2. B), A), A), A), A)

3. B), A), C), A), B)

4. A), A), A), A), A)

Explanation

Correct Answer: 1. C), A), B), A), A)

To start the oneko program and send it to the background, you should use the command oneko &. The ampersand (&) symbol is used to run a command in the background, allowing you to continue using the terminal while the program runs.

To suspend the oneko process, you should press Ctrl + Z. This action sends the current foreground job to the background, pausing its execution. The output will be Suspended.

To check how many jobs you currently have, you should type the command jobs. This command displays a list of jobs currently running in the background or suspended.

To send the suspended oneko job to the background using its job ID, you should use the command bg %1, where %1 is the job ID. The output will confirm the job ID and indicate that the job is running in the background.

Finally, to terminate the oneko job specifying its job ID, you should use the command kill %1. This command sends a termination signal to the specified job, causing it to exit.

Question 53:

Which command displays the static priority of running processes in Linux, and how does it interpret priority values?

A) top; subtracts priority values by 100

B) ps -Al; adds 40 to priority values

C) ps -el; adds 100 to priority values

(Correct)

D) top; adds 50 to priority values

Explanation

The ps command with the -el option displays the static priority of running processes, and it adds 100 to the priority values by default to provide the actual priority.

Question 54:

What range of values does the nice command accept for adjusting process niceness in Linux?

A) -100 to 100

B) -20 to 19

(Correct)

C) -40 to 99

D) 0 to 255

Explanation

The nice command in Linux accepts values ranging from -20 (less nice, higher priority) to 19 (more nice, lower priority) for adjusting process niceness.

Question 55:

Which command is used to change the priority of a running

process in Linux?

A) nice

B) renice

(Correct)

C) top

D) ps

Explanation

The renice command is used to change the priority of a running process in Linux. It can adjust the priority of a specific process identified by its PID.

Question 56:

What does the `-v` option do when used with the `grep` command?

A) Displays the version of `grep`

B) Searches for matches in hidden files

C) Inverts the match, displaying lines that do not match the pattern

(Correct)

D) Counts the total number of matches

Explanation

The `-v` option with the `grep` command inverts the match, displaying lines that do not match the specified pattern.

Question 57:

Which option with the `sed` command is used to replace a match with text?

A) d

B) c

C) a

D) s

(Correct)

Explanation

The `s` command in `sed` is used for substitution, to replace a match with specified text.

Question 58:

How can you display only the parts of a text stream that match a pattern using `grep`?

A) Use the `-n` option

B) Use the `-o` option

(Correct)

C) Use the `-c` option

D) Use the `-i` option

Explanation

The `-o` option with the `grep` command is used to display only the matching parts of a text stream.

Question 59:

Which pseudo-filesystem contains device information and

kernel data related to hardware in Linux?

A) /proc

B) /dev

C) /sys

(Correct)

D) /mnt

Explanation

The /sys directory contains device information and kernel data related to hardware in Linux.

Question 60:

Which option with the `grep` command is used to show the line numbers of matching lines?

A) -i

B) -n

(Correct)

C) -v

D) -c

Explanation

The `-n` option with the `grep` command is used to show the line numbers of matching lines.

Question 61:

What is the purpose of the `:q!` command in vi?

A) Save the changes and quit vi.

B) Quit vi without saving changes.

(Correct)

C) Quit vi and prompt to save changes.

D) Save and quit vi forcibly.

Explanation

The `:q!` command in vi quits the editor without saving any changes made to the document, disregarding any unsaved modifications.

Question 62:

How can a user open a file in vi and jump directly to a specific line?

A) vi +line_number filename

(Correct)

B) vi -line_number filename

C) vi /line_number filename

D) vi *line_number filename

Explanation

To open a file in vi and jump directly to a specific line, the command format is `vi +line_number filename`. This places the cursor at the specified line within the file upon opening.

Question 63:

Which key in vi is used to start recording a macro?

A) q

(Correct)

B) m

C) r

D) Ctrl

Explanation

In vi, pressing the `q` key followed by a register key (e.g., `q` followed by `d` for register `d`) starts recording a macro associated with that register.

Question 64:

What command is used to create an ext4 filesystem on a specific partition?

A) mkfs.ext4

(Correct)

B) mkfs.xfs

C) mkfs.fat

D) mkfs.vfat

Explanation

The command "mkfs.ext4" is used to create an ext4 filesystem.

Question 65:

Which option is used with mkfs.xfs to specify the block size on the filesystem?

A) -m

B) -b

(Correct)

C) -f

D) -q

Explanation

The "-b" option is used with mkfs.xfs to specify the block size on the filesystem.

Question 66:

What is the primary limitation of the FAT filesystem?

A) Maximum file size of 16 exabytes

B) Maximum disk size of 128 petabytes

C) Limited support for long file names

(Correct)

D) Inability to create a bootable filesystem

Explanation

One of the primary limitations of the FAT filesystem is its limited support for long file names.

Question 67:

Which filesystem is commonly used for large capacity flash drives, memory cards, and external disks due to its interoperability across different operating systems?

A) ext4

B) XFS

C) FAT32

(Correct)

D) Btrfs

Explanation

FAT32 is commonly used for large capacity flash drives, memory cards, and external disks due to its interoperability across different operating systems.

Question 68:

What is the purpose of the -c option with mkfs.fat?

A) Create a filesystem with a specific block size

B) Check the target device for bad blocks before creating the filesystem

(Correct)

C) Specify the size of the FAT (File Allocation Table)

D) Set the volume label for the filesystem

Explanation

The "-c" option with mkfs.fat is used to check the target device for bad blocks before creating the filesystem.

Question 69:

Which command is used to repair ext2, ext3, and ext4 filesystems?

A) xfs_repair

B) fsck

C) e2fsck

(Correct)

D) xfs_db

Explanation

The `e2fsck` command is specifically used to repair ext2, ext3, and ext4 filesystems.

Question 70:

Which parameter of the `e2fsck` command automatically attempts to fix any errors found?

A) -N

B) -p

(Correct)

C) -y

D) -f

Explanation

The `-p` parameter of the `e2fsck` command automatically attempts to fix errors found.

Question 71:

What utility is used to fine-tune parameters of ext2, ext3, and ext4 filesystems?

A) tune2fs

(Correct)

B) fsck

C) xfs_repair

D) df

Explanation

The `tune2fs` utility is used to fine-tune parameters of ext2, ext3, and ext4 filesystems.

Question 72:

Which parameter of the `tune2fs` command sets the maximum number of times a filesystem can be mounted before being checked?

A) -c

(Correct)

B) -i

C) -L

D) -U

Explanation

The `-c` parameter of the `tune2fs` command sets the maximum mount count before filesystem check.

Question 73:

What command can be used to list the processes accessing a filesystem in Linux?

A) ps

B) top

C) lsof

(Correct)

D) lsblk

Explanation

The `lsof` command in Linux is used to list the processes that are accessing a filesystem, along with the files that are open.

Question 74:

Which directory is traditionally used as the default mount point for user-removable media in Linux?

A) /mnt

B) /usr

C) /media

(Correct)

D) /home

Explanation

Traditionally, the `/media` directory is used as the default mount point for user-removable media such as external disks, USB flash drives, and memory card readers.

Question 75:

How can you specify the UUID of a filesystem when mounting it in Linux?

A) Using the `-u` parameter with the `mount` command

B) Using the `UUID=` option in the `/etc/fstab` file

(Correct)

C) Using the `-uuid` parameter with the `mount` command

D) Using the `--uuid` option in the `/etc/fstab` file

Explanation

In the `/etc/fstab` file, you can specify the UUID of a filesystem using the `UUID=` option followed by the UUID of the partition.

Question 76:

Which systemd target is typically used to specify when a mount unit should be activated during bootup?

A) graphical.target

B) multi-user.target

(Correct)

C) network.target

D) basic.target

Explanation

The `multi-user.target` in systemd is typically used to specify when a mount unit should be activated during bootup, indicating a normal multi-user system initialization.

Question 77:

What is the octal value for read, write, and execute permissions for the owner, and read-only permissions for the group and others?

A) 755

(Correct)

B) 777

C) 644

D) 666

Explanation

7 corresponds to read, write, and execute permissions, while 5 corresponds to read and execute permissions. Therefore, for the owner: rwx (7), and for group and others: r-x (5).

Question 78:

Which command is used to change the ownership of a file?

A) chown

(Correct)

B) chmod

C) chgrp

D) own

Explanation

The `chown` command is used to change the ownership of a file or directory.

Question 79:

How can you determine whether a file is a hard link or the original file in Linux?

A) Check the size of the file.

B) Use the `ls -li` command and compare inode numbers.

(Correct)

C) Look for the presence of the `-s` flag in the file's permissions.

D) Examine the file's creation date.

Explanation

Hard links and the original file will have the same inode number when listed with the `ls -li` command.

Question 80:

Which of the following statements regarding hard links is true in Linux?

A) Hard links can only be created within the same directory.

B) Hard links preserve the original file's inode.

(Correct)

C) Hard links can traverse different partitions and filesystems.

D) Hard links can be created using the `mv` command.

Explanation

Hard links create additional directory entries pointing to the same inode as the original file, preserving its inode.

Question 81:

What is the significance of the inode count when listing files in a directory in Linux?

A) It represents the number of blocks used by the file.

B) It indicates the number of links pointing to the file.

(Correct)

C) It denotes the file's permission settings.

D) It signifies the file's size in bytes.

Explanation

The inode count represents the number of hard links pointing to the file.

Question 82:

Which command is used to remove a symbolic link in Linux?

A) rm

(Correct)

B) ln -s

C) cp

D) mv

Explanation

The `rm` command is used to remove files, including symbolic links.

Question 83:

Which command displays the full path to an executable file in Linux?

A) whereis

B) type

C) locate

D) which

(Correct)

Explanation

The which command displays the full path to an executable file in Linux.

Question 84:

What does the -iname parameter do in the find command?

A) It searches for files based on specific attributes.

B) It specifies the minimum depth for the search.

C) It performs a case-insensitive search for file names.

(Correct)

D) It restricts the search to specific filesystem types.

Explanation

The -iname parameter in the find command performs a case-insensitive search for file names.

Question 85:

What is the purpose of the /var/tmp directory according to the FHS?

A) To store runtime variable data used by running processes.

B) To provide a mount point for temporarily mounted filesystems.

C) To store temporary files that persist between reboots.

D) To store temporary files that should not be cleared during system boot-up.

(Correct)

Explanation

According to the FHS, the /var/tmp directory is used to store temporary files that should not be cleared during system boot-up.

Question 86:

Which command is used to find the location of manual pages, binaries, and source code on a Linux system?

A) locate

B) which

C) whereis

(Correct)

D) type

Explanation

The whereis command is used to find the location of manual pages, binaries, and source code on a Linux system.

Question 87:

What does the -t parameter do in the type command?

A) It displays the location of a binary.

B) It displays all pathnames that match the executable.

C) It shows the file type of the command.

(Correct)

D) It filters the results to only show binaries.

Explanation

The -t parameter in the type command shows the file type of the command, which can be alias, keyword, function, builtin, or file.

Question 88:

What is the parameter for chmod in symbolic mode to enable the sticky bit on a directory?

A) +t

(Correct)

B) +s

C) +x

D) +k

Explanation

The sticky bit is represented by `+t` in symbolic mode for chmod.

Question 89:

Imagine there is a file named document.txt in the directory /home/carol/Documents. What is the command to create a symbolic link to it named text.txt on the current directory?

A) ln -s /home/carol/Documents/document.txt text.txt

B) ln -s document.txt /home/carol/Documents/text.txt

C) ln -s /home/carol/Documents/text.txt

D) ln -s text.txt /home/carol/Documents/document.txt

(Correct)

Explanation

The correct syntax for creating a symbolic link is `ln -s <target> <link_name>`.

Question 90:

A file called test.sh has the following permissions: -rwsr-xr-x, meaning the SUID bit is set. Now, run the following commands:

$ chmod u-x test.sh

$ ls -l test.sh

rwSr-xr-x 1 carol carol 33 Dec 11 10:36 test.sh

What did we do? What does the uppercase S mean?

A) We removed execute permission for the owner; the uppercase S indicates the setuid bit is still set.

(Correct)

B) We removed execute permission for the owner; the uppercase S indicates the setgid bit is set.

C) We removed execute permission for the owner; the uppercase S indicates no special permissions are set.

D) We removed execute permission for the owner; the uppercase S indicates the sticky bit is set.

Explanation

The uppercase `S` in the owner's execute permission slot indicates that the setuid bit is set but the execute permission for the owner has been removed.

PRACTICE TEST THREE - LPIC-1 EXAM 101 VERSION: 5.0

90 questions | 2 hours | 90% correct required to pass

The LPIC-1 Exam 101 Version: 5.0 Practice Test is a comprehensive resource designed to prepare you for the LPIC-1 (Linux Professional Institute Certification) Exam 101. It includes practice questions that mimic the format and content of the actual test. Each **Question** comes with a detailed **Explanation** to help you understand the concepts better. This practice test is an excellent tool to harness the power of Linux and achieve LPIC-1 certification.

Question 1:

What is the purpose of the file /etc/modprobe.d/blacklist.conf in Linux?

A) To list all currently loaded kernel modules.

B) To store parameters for kernel modules.

C) To block the loading of specific kernel modules.

((**Correct**))

D) To create new kernel modules.

Explanation

The file /etc/modprobe.d/blacklist.conf is used to block the loading of specific kernel modules in Linux.

Question 2:

Which directory contains files associated with system devices, particularly storage devices, in Linux?

A) /proc

B) /dev

((**Correct**))

C) /sys

D) /mnt

Explanation

The /dev directory contains files associated with system devices, particularly storage devices, in Linux.

Question 3:

How are storage devices identified in Linux kernel version 2.4 onwards?

A) By using the device manufacturer's name.

B) By using the device type (e.g., IDE, SATA, SCSI) and partitions.

((**Correct**))

C) By using random alphanumeric identifiers.

D) By using sequential numbers starting from 1.

Explanation

Storage devices in Linux kernel version 2.4 onwards are identified by using the device type (e.g., IDE, SATA, SCSI) and partitions.

Question 4:

What is the primary function of the BIOS in the boot process of an x86 system?

A) Execute system initialization scripts

B) Load the kernel into RAM

C) Activate basic hardware components

((**Correct**))

D) Mount filesystems

Explanation

The BIOS activates basic hardware components to initialize the system, including storage media and input/output devices.

Question 5:

Which runlevels are shared between all distributions based on the SysVinit standard?

A) Runlevels 1 and 2

B) Runlevels 2 and 3

C) Runlevels 0, 1, and 6

((**Correct**))

D) Runlevels 3, 4, and 5

Explanation

Runlevels 0 (halt), 1 (single-user mode), and 6 (reboot) are shared between all distributions based on the SysVinit standard.

Question 6:

What is the purpose of the `maxcpus` kernel parameter?

A) Set the root partition

B) Limit the number of visible processors

((**Correct**))

C) Enable/disable ACPI support

D) Hide most boot messages

Explanation

The `maxcpus` kernel parameter is used to limit the number of processors visible to the system in symmetric multiprocessor machines.

Question 7:

Which command displays a list of available boot numbers and their corresponding timestamps in a systemd-based Linux system?

A) bootctl --list

B) systemctl --boot

C) journalctl --list-boots

((**Correct**))

D) dmesg --boots

Explanation

The `journalctl --list-boots` command displays a list of available boot numbers and their corresponding timestamps in a systemd-based Linux system.

Question 8:

Which runlevel is equivalent to single user mode in a SysVinit system?

A) Runlevel 0

B) Runlevel 1

((**Correct**))

C) Runlevel 3

D) Runlevel 5

Explanation

Runlevel 1 is equivalent to single user mode in a SysVinit system.

Question 9:

Which command is used to set the default runlevel in a SysVinit system?

A) telinit

((**Correct**))

B) initctl

C) systemctl

D) runlevel

Explanation

The telinit command is used to set the default runlevel in a SysVinit system.

Question 10:

Which type of systemd unit is responsible for grouping other units and managing them as a single unit?

A) service

B) target

((**Correct**))

C) socket

D) device

Explanation

A target unit in systemd is responsible for grouping other units and managing them as a single unit.

Question 11:

What does the command `shutdown -r now` do in a SysVinit system?

A) Puts the system in low power mode

B) Shuts down the system

C) Restarts the system immediately

((**Correct**))

D) Sends a warning message to all logged-in users

Explanation

The `shutdown -r now` command in a SysVinit system restarts the system immediately.

Question 12:

What happens if a filesystem is mounted on a directory that already contains files?

A) The existing files will be deleted.

B) The existing files will be overwritten.

C) The existing files will be inaccessible until unmounted.

((**Correct**))

D) The existing files will be moved to the root directory.

Explanation

If a filesystem is mounted on a directory that already contains files, those files will be inaccessible until the filesystem is unmounted.

Question 13:

Which type of partition table is used for disks on machines running the Unified Extensible Firmware Interface (UEFI)?

A) MBR

B) GPT

((**Correct**))

C) FAT

D) LBA

Explanation

Disks on machines running UEFI use the GUID Partition Table (GPT) format for partitioning.

Question 14:

Which directory contains system logs, temporary files, and cached application data in Linux?

A) /tmp

B) /home

C) /var

((**Correct**))

D) /etc

Explanation

The /var directory in Linux contains system logs, temporary files, and cached application data.

Question 15:

How are Logical Volumes (LVs) identified in Linux?

A) /dev/VGNAME/LVNAME

((**Correct**))

B) /mnt/LVNAME

C) /var/LVNAME

D) /home/LVNAME

Explanation

Logical Volumes (LVs) in Linux are identified by the path /dev/VGNAME/LVNAME, where VGNAME is the name of the Volume Group and LVNAME is the name of the Logical Volume.

Question 16:

How can custom menu entries be added to GRUB Legacy and GRUB 2?

A) By editing the /boot/grub/grub.cfg file directly.

B) By editing the /etc/default/grub file.

C) By editing the /boot/grub/menu.lst file.

((**Correct**))

D) By running the grub-install command.

Explanation

Custom menu entries can be added to GRUB Legacy and GRUB 2 by editing the /boot/grub/menu.lst file.

Question 17:

What command can be used to enter the GRUB 2 shell during the boot process?

A) Ctrl + C

B) Ctrl + X

C) E

D) C

((**Correct**))

Explanation

The command to enter the GRUB 2 shell during the boot process is C.

Question 18:

What does the `makeactive` command do in GRUB Legacy?

A) Sets a flag indicating that the partition is active.

((**Correct**))

B) Installs GRUB Legacy on the disk.

C) Loads the kernel image.

D) Edits the GRUB configuration file.

Explanation

The `makeactive` command in GRUB Legacy sets a flag indicating that the partition is active, which is necessary for booting.

Question 19:

How can GRUB Legacy be installed from a GRUB shell?

A) Using the setup command.

((**Correct**))

B) Using the fdisk command.

C) Using the install command.

D) Using the mount command.

Explanation

GRUB Legacy can be installed from a GRUB shell using the setup command.

Question 20:

What is the purpose of the symbolic link pointing to a shared library file in Linux?

A) To duplicate the library file

B) To redirect library calls to the actual file

((**Correct**))

C) To hide the library file

D) To rename the library file

Explanation

The correct answer is B) The symbolic link points to the actual shared library file, allowing the system to locate and use it.

Question 21:

Which file contains the include line for *.conf files in the /etc/ld.so.conf.d directory?

A) /etc/ld.so.conf

((**Correct**))

B) /etc/ld.so.cache

C) /etc/ld.so.conf.d/main.conf

D) /etc/ld.so.conf.d/include.conf

Explanation

The correct answer is A) The file /etc/ld.so.conf contains the include line for *.conf files in the /etc/ld.so.conf.d directory.

Question 22:

What command is used to print the lists of directories and candidate libraries stored in the current cache file of shared library paths?

A) `ldconfig -v`

B) `ldconfig -p`

((**Correct**))

C) `ldconfig -u`

D) `ldconfig -c`

Explanation

The correct answer is B) The `ldconfig -p` command is used to print the lists of directories and candidate libraries stored in the current cache file of shared library paths.

Question 23:

What does the "apt-cache search" command do?

A) Updates the package index

B) Installs a package

C) Searches for packages in the package index

((**Correct**))

D) Removes a package

Explanation

The "search" parameter is used with apt-cache to search for packages in the package index.

Question 24:

How can you list all installed packages on your system using dpkg?

A) dpkg -i

B) dpkg --get-selections

((**Correct**))

C) dpkg -L

D) dpkg -r

Explanation

The "--get-selections" parameter is used with dpkg to list all installed packages on the system.

Question 25:

Which command is used to upgrade all installed packages to the latest versions available from the repositories?

A) apt-get update

B) apt-get upgrade

C) apt-get dist-upgrade

((**Correct**))

D) apt-get install

Explanation

The "dist-upgrade" parameter is used with apt-get to upgrade all installed packages to the latest versions.

Question 26:

How can you add a new repository with `zypper`?

A) `zypper add-repo URL`

((**Correct**))

B) `zypper create-repo URL`

C) `zypper import-repo URL`

D) `zypper new-repo URL`

Explanation

The `add-repo` option with `zypper` is used to add a new repository.

Question 27:

What is the purpose of the `zypper refresh` command?

A) To update the package index

((**Correct**))

B) To install new packages

C) To remove outdated packages

D) To clean the package cache

Explanation

The `refresh` option with `zypper` updates the package index to ensure it includes the latest package information.

Question 28:

How can you remove a repository with `zypper`?

A) `zypper remove-repo REPO`

B) `zypper delete-repo REPO`

C) `zypper disable-repo REPO`

D) `zypper removerepo REPO`

((**Correct**))

Explanation

The `removerepo` option with `zypper` is used to remove a repository.

Question 29:

Which package management tool is primarily used on SUSE Linux and openSUSE?

A) yum

B) dnf

C) zypper

((**Correct**))

D) rpm

Explanation

`zypper` is the package management tool primarily used on SUSE Linux and openSUSE distributions.

Question 30:

What is the purpose of the D-Bus machine ID in a Linux installation?

A) To identify the physical hardware of the machine

B) To manage network configurations

C) To facilitate communication between different applications

D) To uniquely identify each virtual machine running on a hypervisor

((**Correct**))

Explanation

D) The D-Bus machine ID is used to uniquely identify each virtual machine running on a hypervisor.

Question 31:

Which container technology provides an isolated environment for running applications with reduced overhead?

A) Docker

((**Correct**))

B) Kubernetes

C) LXD/LXC

D) systemd-nspawn

Explanation

Docker provides isolated environments for running

applications with reduced overhead compared to virtual machines.

Question 32:

What is the main benefit of using containers over virtual machines?

A) Containers provide full isolation of resources.

B) Containers allow for easier migration between hypervisors.

C) Containers have lower overhead and faster deployment compared to virtual machines.

((**Correct**))

D) Containers have better hardware emulation capabilities.

Explanation

Containers have lower overhead and faster deployment compared to virtual machines, making them more efficient for certain applications.

Question 33:

Which command is used to list all environment variables in Linux?

A) `vars`

B) `listenv`

C) `printenv`

((**Correct**))

D) `envlist`

Explanation

The correct answer is C) `printenv`. This command lists all environment variables and their values.

Question 34:

What is the purpose of the `export` command in Linux?

A) To import environment variables

B) To list environment variables

C) To unset environment variables

D) To pass environment variables to child shells

((**Correct**))

Explanation

The correct answer is D) To pass environment variables to child shells. The `export` command is used to make environment variables available to child processes.

Question 35:

How can you create a new file with a name containing spaces in Linux?

A) `touch "file name"`

((**Correct**))

B) `touch file\ name`

C) `touch 'file name'`

D) `touch file-name`

Explanation

The correct answer is A) `touch "file name"`. Using double quotes allows for the creation of a file with spaces in its name.

Question 36:

What is the purpose of the `sed` command in Linux?

A) To display the contents of a file.

B) To search for patterns within files.

C) To edit files using pre-defined patterns.

((**Correct**))

D) To compress files.

Explanation

The correct answer is C) The `sed` command is a stream editor used to edit files using pre-defined patterns.

Question 37:

Which command is used to paginate the contents of a file and allows for navigation and search functionality?

A) `head`

B) `tail`

C) `less`

((**Correct**))

D) `more`

Explanation

The correct answer is C) The `less` command paginates the contents of a file and allows for navigation and search functionality.

Question 38:

Which command is used to copy data from one location to another in Linux?

A) cp

B) mv

C) mkdir

D) dd

((**Correct**))

Explanation

The correct answer is A) cp.

Option A) cp is the command used to copy data from one location to another in Linux. Let's delve into the explanation:

cp: This is the command used to copy files and directories in Linux. It allows you to duplicate files and directories from one location to another.

When you execute cp source destination, the cp command copies the contents of the source file or directory to the destination location. If the destination is an existing directory, the source file or directory is copied into it. If the destination is a filename, the source file is copied and renamed to the destination filename.

Now, let's briefly discuss the other options:

mv: This command is used to move files and directories from

one location to another. It effectively relocates the file or directory instead of creating a duplicate.

mkdir: This command is used to create directories, not to copy data.

dd: This command is used for low-level copying and conversion of data, often used for tasks such as creating disk images or cloning drives. While it can be used for copying data, it's not typically used for general file copying operations.

Therefore, option A) cp is the correct choice as it represents the command used to copy data from one location to another in Linux.

Question 39:

Which command is used to remove a directory in Linux?

A) rm

B) rmdir

((**Correct**))

C) cp

D) mv

Explanation

The correct answer is B) rmdir.

Option B) rmdir is the command used to remove a directory in Linux. Let's delve into the explanation:

rmdir: This command removes an empty directory in Linux. It cannot be used to remove directories that contain files or other directories. It's specifically designed for deleting empty directories.

When you execute rmdir directory_name, the rmdir command deletes the specified directory if it is empty. If the directory contains any files or subdirectories, the rmdir command will fail with an error message.

Now, let's briefly discuss the other options:

rm: This command is used to remove files and directories in Linux. However, to remove a directory with files or subdirectories, you typically need to use the -r or --recursive option with rm, which allows recursive removal of directories and their contents.

cp: This command is used to copy files and directories, not to remove them.

mv: This command is used to move or rename files and directories, not to remove them.

Therefore, option B) rmdir is the correct choice as it represents the command used to remove a directory in Linux.

Question 40:

Consider the listing below:

$ ls -lh

total 60K

drwxr-xr-x 2 frank frank 4.0K Apr 1 2018 Desktop

drwxr-xr-x 2 frank frank 4.0K Apr 1 2018 Documents

What does the character d represent in the output?

A) The files are directories.

(**(Correct)**)

B) The files are hidden.

C) The files are executable.

D) The files are symbolic links.

Explanation

The 'd' in the first column indicates that the listed items are directories.

Question 41:

Consider the listing below:

$ ls -lh

total 60K

drwxr-xr-x 2 frank frank 4.0K Apr 1 2018 Desktop

drwxr-xr-x 2 frank frank 4.0K Apr 1 2018 Documents

Why are the sizes given in human readable format?

A) To save disk space.

B) To make them easier to read.

(**(Correct)**)

C) To enhance security.

D) To increase performance.

Explanation

Sizes are displayed in human-readable format (e.g., 4.0K, 8.8K) to make them easier for users to understand at a glance.

Question 42:

Consider the listing below: $ ls -lh total 60K drwxr-xr-x 2 frank

frank 4.0K Apr 1 2018 Desktop drwxr-xr-x 2 frank frank 4.0K Apr 1 2018 Documents - What would be the difference in the output if ls was used with no argument?

A) It would list only directories.

B) It would list all files and directories in the current directory.

((**Correct**))

C) It would list only hidden files.

D) It would list only executable files.

Explanation

Without any arguments, the `ls` command lists all files and directories in the current directory.

Question 43:

What should be used as the separator when using the -print0 option with the find command in Linux?

A) Tab

B) Newline

C) Null character

((**Correct**))

D) Space

Explanation

The "-print0" option with the find command in Linux uses a null character as the separator.

Question 44:

How can you redirect the standard error (stderr) of a process to the standard input (stdin) of another process in Linux?

A) Using the > operator

B) Using the < operator

C) Using the 2>&1 operator

((**Correct**))

D) Using the | operator

Explanation

In Linux, you can redirect the standard error (stderr) of a process to the standard input (stdin) of another process using the "2>&1" operator.

Question 45:

In addition to text files, the command `cat` can also work with binary data, like sending the contents of a block device to a file. Using redirection, how can `cat` send the contents of device `/dev/sdc` to the file `sdc.img` in the current directory?

A) `cat /dev/sdc > sdc.img`

((**Correct**))

B) `cat /dev/sdc < sdc.img`

C) `cat /dev/sdc >> sdc.img`

D) `cat sdc.img < /dev/sdc`

Explanation

The `>` redirection operator is used to send the output of

`cat /dev/sdc` to the file `sdc.img`.

Question 46:

What's the name of the standard channel redirected by the command `date 1> now.txt`?

A) Standard Output (STDOUT)

((**Correct**))

B) Standard Error (STDERR)

C) Standard Input (STDIN)

D) Standard Descriptor (STDDESC)

Explanation

The `1>` redirection sends the standard output (STDOUT) of the `date` command to the file `now.txt`.

Question 47:

After trying to overwrite a file using redirection, a user gets an error informing that option noclobber is enabled. How can the option noclobber be deactivated for the current session?

A) `set +o noclobber`

((**Correct**))

B) `set -o noclobber`

C) `unset +o noclobber`

D) `unset -o noclobber`

Explanation

The `set +o noclobber` command deactivates the

`noclobber` option for the current session, allowing file overwriting.

Question 48:

Discover the PIDs of all the processes spawned by the Apache HTTPD web server (apache2) with two different commands: Which commands correctly retrieve the PIDs of Apache HTTPD processes?

A) pidof apache2 and pgrep apache2

((**Correct**))

B) ps aux | grep apache2 and top | grep apache2

C) apache2 -p and netstat -p apache2

D) ps -e | grep apache2 and top -p apache2

Explanation

The correct answer is A) pidof apache2 and pgrep apache2.

Option A) provides two commands that correctly retrieve the PIDs of Apache HTTPD processes:

pidof apache2: This command retrieves the PID (Process ID) of the Apache HTTPD process directly. It is specifically designed to find the PID of a running process by its name.

pgrep apache2: This command searches for the process whose name matches the pattern provided (in this case, "apache2") and returns its PID. It is a versatile command-line tool for finding processes based on various criteria, including process name.

Now, let's briefly discuss the other options:

B) ps aux | grep apache2 and top | grep apache2: These

commands use ps and top to list running processes and then filter the output using grep to find lines containing "apache2". While they can find Apache HTTPD processes, they are less direct and may include additional processes that contain "apache2" in their name or command-line arguments.

apache2 -p and netstat -p apache2: These commands are incorrect. apache2 -p does not retrieve PIDs; it is used to specify a process ID in Apache HTTPD's configuration file. netstat -p apache2 is also incorrect as netstat does not accept a process name as an argument.

ps -e | grep apache2 and top -p apache2: These commands use ps and top to list all running processes and then filter the output using grep to find lines containing "apache2". Similar to option B, while they can find Apache HTTPD processes, they are less direct and may include additional processes.

Therefore, option A) pidof apache2 and pgrep apache2 provides the correct commands to retrieve the PIDs of Apache HTTPD processes.

Question 49:

Terminate all apache2 processes without using their PIDs and with two different commands: How can you terminate all Apache HTTPD processes without specifying their PIDs?

A) killall apache2 and pkill apache2

((**Correct**))

B) kill apache2 and stop apache2

C) terminate apache2 and kill -all apache2

D) killall -p apache2 and stop -p apache2

Explanation

The correct answer is A) killall apache2 and pkill apache2.

Option A) provides two commands that correctly terminate all Apache HTTPD processes without specifying their PIDs:

killall apache2: This command sends the SIGTERM signal to all processes named "apache2", causing them to gracefully terminate. It is specifically designed to kill processes by their name.

pkill apache2: This command searches for processes whose name matches the pattern provided (in this case, "apache2") and sends them the SIGTERM signal to terminate them. Similar to killall, it provides a more targeted approach to terminating processes by name.

Now, let's briefly discuss the other options:

B) kill apache2 and stop apache2: These commands are incorrect. kill apache2 is not a valid command; you must specify either a PID or a signal to send to the process. stop apache2 is also incorrect; there is no standard Linux command named "stop" for terminating processes.

C) terminate apache2 and kill -all apache2: These commands are incorrect. terminate apache2 is not a valid command; there is no such command in Linux. kill -all apache2 is also incorrect; the correct syntax for killing processes by name using kill is killall, not kill -all.

D) killall -p apache2 and stop -p apache2: These commands are incorrect. killall -p apache2 is invalid syntax; the -p option with killall is used to specify a parent process ID, not to terminate processes by name. stop -p apache2 is also invalid; there is no standard Linux command named "stop" with a -p option.

Therefore, option A) killall apache2 and pkill apache2 provides the correct commands to terminate all Apache HTTPD processes without specifying their PIDs.

Question 50:

Suppose you have to terminate all instances of apache2 and you do not have time to find out what their PIDs are. How would you accomplish that using kill with the default SIGTERM signal in a one-liner: Which command can effectively terminate all instances of Apache HTTPD with the default SIGTERM signal?

A) killall -15 apache2

B) killall -SIGTERM apache2

C) killall -9 apache2

D) killall apache2

((**Correct**))

Explanation

The correct answer is D) killall apache2.

Option D) provides the correct command to terminate all instances of Apache HTTPD with the default SIGTERM signal. Let's delve into the explanation:

killall: This command is used to terminate processes by name in Linux.

apache2: This is the name of the process to be terminated.

When you execute killall apache2, the command sends the SIGTERM signal to all processes named "apache2", causing them to gracefully terminate. SIGTERM is the default signal sent by killall when no signal is specified, and it is commonly used for gracefully terminating processes, allowing them to clean up resources before exiting.

Now, let's briefly discuss the other options:

killall -15 apache2: This command is equivalent to killall -SIGTERM apache2, where -15 represents the SIGTERM signal. While it specifies SIGTERM explicitly, it is unnecessary as SIGTERM is the default signal used by killall.

killall -SIGTERM apache2: This command explicitly specifies the SIGTERM signal using the -SIGTERM option. While it achieves the same result as option D, it is less concise.

killall -9 apache2: This command sends the SIGKILL signal (signal number 9) to all processes named "apache2". SIGKILL is a harsh signal that immediately terminates processes without allowing them to clean up resources. It is generally not recommended for normal termination as it can lead to data loss or other issues.

Therefore, option D) killall apache2 provides the most straightforward and effective command to terminate all instances of Apache HTTPD with the default SIGTERM signal.

Question 51:

Start top and interact with it by performing the following: Show a forest view of processes:

A) Press Shift + H

((**Correct**))

B) Press F

C) Press Ctrl + F

D) Press Ctrl + T

Explanation

The correct answer is A) Press Shift + H.

Option A) Shift + H is the key combination used to toggle the display of the hierarchical (forest) view of processes in the top command. Let's delve into the explanation:

Shift + H: This key combination toggles the display between the standard process view and the forest (hierarchical) view in top. When you press Shift + H, top switches to the forest view, showing parent-child relationships between processes.

Now, let's briefly discuss the other options:

B) Press F: This key is used to enter the top command's interactive mode, allowing users to toggle the display of fields. It is not used specifically to show the forest view of processes.

Press Ctrl + F: This key combination is not associated with showing the forest view of processes in top. It is not a valid option for this action.

Press Ctrl + T: This key combination is not associated with showing the forest view of processes in top. It is not a valid option for this action.

Therefore, option A) Press Shift + H is the correct choice as it represents the key combination used to show the forest view of processes in the top command.

Question 52:

While running top, show full paths of processes differentiating between userspace and kernelspace:

A) Press Shift + K

B) Press Shift + F

(**(Correct)**)

C) Press F

D) Press Ctrl + U

Explanation

Answer: (B) Press Shift + F

Explanation:

The top command provides various options to customize the displayed information:

Full Paths: By default, top truncates process names for a more compact view. Pressing Shift + F (or sometimes just F) opens a menu for selecting display fields. Use the arrow keys to navigate and choose "COMMAND by PID/TID" (or similar depending on your system). This will display the full path of each process.

User-space vs. Kernel-space: Unfortunately, top doesn't directly differentiate between user-space and kernel-space processes. However, some clues can help:

Processes with system users (like root) often indicate kernel-space processes.

Processes with longer paths typically point to executables on the system, suggesting user-space programs.

Here's a breakdown of the other options and why they're incorrect:

A) Press Shift + K: This key combination typically doesn't exist in top.

C) Press F: While F might open the menu in some systems, using Shift + F is more consistent across various Linux distributions.

D) Press Ctrl + U: This key combination usually refreshes

the top display, not modifying process information.

Question 53:

What command in Linux allows continuous monitoring of processes and enables users to modify process niceness interactively?

A) nice

B) renice

C) ps

D) top

((**Correct**))

Explanation

The top command in Linux allows continuous monitoring of processes and enables users to interactively modify process niceness by selecting a process and adjusting its priority.

Question 54:

What does a negative nice value indicate in the output of the top command in Linux?

A) Lower priority for real-time processes

B) Higher priority for normal processes

C) Lower priority for normal processes

D) Higher priority for real-time processes

((**Correct**))

Explanation

In the output of the top command, a negative nice value indicates a higher priority for real-time processes, as all real-time priorities are displayed as negative numbers.

Question 55:

Which user is typically allowed to decrease the niceness of a process below zero in Linux?

A) Any user

B) Root user

((**Correct**))

C) Regular users with sudo privileges

D) Users belonging to the same group as the process owner

Explanation

In Linux, only the root user is typically allowed to decrease the niceness of a process below zero, enabling the adjustment of process priorities to higher values.

Question 56:

What is the purpose of the `egrep` command in Linux?

A) To search for patterns using basic regular expressions

B) To search for patterns using extended regular expressions

((**Correct**))

C) To search for patterns in binary files

D) To search for patterns in encrypted files

Explanation

The `egrep` command is equivalent to `grep -E` and is used to search for patterns using extended regular expressions.

Question 57:

Which command can be used to search for text in files and perform complex text mining procedures?

A) `ls`

B) `cat`

C) `grep`

((**Correct**))

D) `mv`

Explanation

The `grep` command in Linux is specifically designed for searching text files and can be used for complex text mining procedures when combined with other commands like `sed`.

Question 58:

What does the `-iregex` option do when used with the `find` command?

A) Specifies a regular expression file

B) Performs a case-insensitive search using regular expressions

((**Correct**))

C) Prints the line numbers of matching lines

D) Inverts the match, displaying lines that do not match the pattern

Explanation

The `-iregex` option with the `find` command performs a case-insensitive search using regular expressions.

Question 59:

What extended regular expression would match any email address, like info@example.org?

A) `^[a-zA-Z0-9._%+-]+@[a-zA-Z0-9.-]+\.[a-zA-Z]{2,}$`

((**Correct**))

B) `^[a-zA-Z0-9._%+-]+@[a-zA-Z0-9.-]+\.+[a-zA-Z]{2,}$`

C) `^[a-zA-Z0-9._%+-]+@[a-zA-Z0-9.-]+\.[a-zA-Z0-9.-]+$`

D) `^[a-zA-Z0-9._%+-]+@[a-zA-Z0-9.-]+\.[a-zA-Z]{2,3}$`

Explanation

This regular expression matches any email address with the format `local-part@domain`, where the local part can contain alphanumeric characters, dots, underscores, percentage signs, plus signs, and hyphens, and the domain part consists of alphanumeric characters, dots, and hyphens, with at least two characters for the top-level domain.

Question 60:

What command in vi is used to copy text?

A) y

((**Correct**))

B) c

C) p

D) d

Explanation

In vi, the `y` command is used to copy (or "yank") text. It can be used with various motion commands to copy specific portions of text.

Question 61:

Which key combination in nano is used to start a new selection?

A) Ctrl-6

((**Correct**))

B) Ctrl-K

C) Ctrl-U

D) Meta-6

Explanation

In nano, pressing Ctrl-6 (or Meta-A) starts a new selection, allowing the user to mark a range of text for copying or cutting.

Question 62:

What is the purpose of the `:s/REGEX/TEXT/g` command in vi?

A) Save the changes and quit vi.

B) Search and replace text using a regular expression.

((**Correct**))

C) Go back to navigation mode.

D) Close vi without saving changes.

Explanation

The `:s/REGEX/TEXT/g` command in vi is used to search for occurrences of a regular expression (REGEX) in the current line and replace them with specified text (TEXT).

Question 63:

Which filesystem was created by Microsoft in 2006 to address the limitations of FAT32, specifically regarding file and disk size?

A) NTFS

B) exFAT

((**Correct**))

C) HFS+

D) ext4

Explanation

exFAT was created by Microsoft in 2006 to address the limitations of FAT32 regarding file and disk size.

Question 64:

What command is used to set the volume label for an exFAT filesystem?

A) mklabel

B) mkfs.exfat

((**Correct**))

C) label

D) mkfs.vfat

Explanation

The command "mkfs.exfat" is used to create an exFAT filesystem, and it includes an option to set the volume label.

Question 65:

Which partitioning scheme should be used to partition a 3 TB hard disk into three 1 GB partitions? Why?

A) MBR, because it supports partition sizes up to 2 TB.

B) GPT, because it supports partition sizes larger than 2 TB.

((**Correct**))

C) MBR, because it's the default partitioning scheme.

D) GPT, because it's the legacy partitioning scheme.

Explanation

GPT (GUID Partition Table) should be used because it supports larger partition sizes, making it suitable for a 3 TB hard disk.

Question 66:

On gdisk, how can we find out how much space is available on the disk?

A) Press the `?` key.

((**Correct**))

B) Type `free` and press Enter.

C) Type ` df ` and press Enter.

D) Type ` p ` and press Enter.

Explanation

Pressing the ` ? ` key in ` gdisk ` displays a help menu, which includes information about available commands and options.

Question 67:

What would be the command to create an ext3 filesystem, checking for bad blocks before, with the label MyDisk and a random UUID, on the device /dev/sdc1?

A) ` mkfs.ext3 -c -L MyDisk -U random /dev/sdc1 `

((**Correct**))

B) ` mkfs.ext3 -B -l MyDisk -U random /dev/sdc1 `

C) ` mkfs.ext3 -c -n MyDisk -U random /dev/sdc1 `

D) ` mkfs.ext3 -B -L MyDisk -U random /dev/sdc1 `

Explanation

The ` -c ` option checks for bad blocks before creating the filesystem, ` -L ` sets the label to MyDisk, ` -U random ` generates a random UUID, and ` /dev/sdc1 ` specifies the device.

Question 68:

What command is used to check and repair XFS filesystems?

A) fsck

B) xfs_db

C) xfs_repair

((**Correct**))

D) df

Explanation

The `xfs_repair` command is used to check and repair XFS filesystems.

Question 69:

Which parameter of the `xfs_repair` command scans the filesystem for damage but does not make repairs?

A) -f

B) -d

C) -n

((**Correct**))

D) -v

Explanation

The `-n` parameter of the `xfs_repair` command scans the filesystem but does not make repairs.

Question 70:

What utility is used to view various parameters of an XFS filesystem?

A) fsck

B) xfs_fsr

C) xfs_repair

D) xfs_db

((**Correct**))

Explanation

The `xfs_db` utility is used to view various parameters of an XFS filesystem.

Question 71:

Which command is used to defragment an XFS filesystem?

A) fsck

B) xfs_fsr

((**Correct**))

C) xfs_repair

D) xfs_db

Explanation

The `xfs_fsr` command is used to defragment an XFS filesystem.

Question 72:

What file extension is used for systemd mount unit files?

A) .service

B) .target

C) .mount

((**Correct**))

D) .automount

Explanation

Systemd mount unit files use the `.mount` file extension.

Question 73:

How can you enable an automount unit to activate on every boot in systemd?

A) By using the `--enable` option with the `systemctl` command

B) By adding the unit file to the `/etc/systemd/system` directory

C) By using the `enable` directive in the automount unit file

((**Correct**))

D) By using the `WantedBy` directive in the automount unit file

Explanation

In the automount unit file, you can use the `enable` directive to specify that the unit should be enabled, meaning it will activate on every boot.

Question 74:

Which command is used to reload systemd configuration files after making changes?

A) systemctl reload

B) systemctl restart

C) systemctl daemon-reload

((**Correct**))

D) systemctl update

Explanation

The `systemctl daemon-reload` command is used to reload systemd configuration files after making changes.

Question 75:

What is the purpose of the `fstab` file in Linux?

A) To list all filesystems currently mounted

B) To store system configuration settings related to filesystems

((**Correct**))

C) To list all available filesystem types

D) To track filesystem usage statistics

Explanation

The `fstab` file in Linux is used to store system configuration settings related to filesystems, including mount points, types, options, etc.

Question 76:

What does the sticky bit do when set on a directory?

A) Prevents users from removing or renaming a file unless they own the file or directory.

((**Correct**))

B) Makes the process run with the privileges of the group who owns the file.

C) Makes every file or directory created under it inherit the group from the parent directory.

D) Has no effect on directories.

Explanation

The sticky bit on directories prevents users from removing or renaming a file unless they own the file or directory.

Question 77:

In symbolic mode, what does the parameter `g+s` do with the `chmod` command?

A) Grants execute permissions to the group.

B) Revokes execute permissions from the group.

C) Sets the SGID bit, making the process run with the privileges of the group who owns the file.

((**Correct**))

D) Sets the sticky bit on the file.

Explanation

In symbolic mode, `g+s` sets the SGID bit, which makes the process run with the privileges of the group who owns the file.

Question 78:

In Linux, how can you ensure that a symbolic link remains valid even if the target file is moved?

A) By using the `-f` flag with the `ln` command.

B) By specifying the full path to the target file when creating the symbolic link.

((**Correct**))

C) By creating the symbolic link in the same directory as the target file.

D) By setting the permissions of the symbolic link to read-only.

Explanation

Specifying the full path ensures that the symbolic link remains valid regardless of the location of the target file.

Question 79:

Which of the following statements regarding symbolic links is true in Linux?

A) Symbolic links preserve the original file's inode.

B) Symbolic links cannot be created across different partitions.

((**Correct**))

C) Symbolic links are indicated by an 'h' as the first character in the permissions field.

D) Symbolic links point directly to the target file's data blocks.

Explanation

Symbolic links can traverse different partitions and filesystems, unlike hard links.

Question 80:

How does the behavior of hard links differ from symbolic links when the target file is moved in Linux?

A) Hard links become invalid, while symbolic links remain intact.

B) Hard links automatically update their target location, while symbolic links become invalid.

C) Both hard links and symbolic links become invalid.

D) Both hard links and symbolic links remain intact.

((**Correct**))

Explanation

Both hard links and symbolic links remain valid even if the target file is moved.

Question 81:

Which command is used to view the inode number of files in a directory listing in Linux?

A) ls -l

B) ls -i

((**Correct**))

C) ls -a

D) ls -lh

Explanation

The `-i` option with the `ls` command is used to display the inode number of files in a directory listing.

Question 82:

Explain the difference between a hard link to a file and a copy of this file.

A) A hard link shares the same inode and data blocks with

the original file, while a copy is a separate file with a different inode and data blocks.

((**Correct**))

B) A hard link is a duplicate of the original file, while a copy is a reference to the original file.

C) A hard link points to the original file, while a copy duplicates the original file's content.

D) A hard link creates a shortcut to the original file, while a copy creates a new file with the same content.

Explanation

Hard links and copies are two different ways of creating duplicates of a file. Hard links share the same inode and data blocks, meaning they point directly to the same data. Copies, on the other hand, create entirely separate files with their own inodes and data blocks.

Question 83:

Imagine that inside a directory you create a file called recipes.txt. Inside this directory, you will also create a hard link to this file, called receitas.txt, and a symbolic (or soft) link to this called rezepte.txt.

$ touch recipes.txt

$ ln recipes.txt receitas.txt

$ ln -s recipes.txt rezepte.txt

What would happen to the soft link rezepte.txt if the file receitas.txt is deleted? Why?

A) rezepte.txt will become a copy of recipes.txt.

B) rezepte.txt will be automatically deleted.

C) rezepte.txt will become a dangling link.

((**Correct**))

D) rezepte.txt will retain its symbolic link to recipes.txt.

Explanation

If the file `receitas.txt` (the target of `rezepte.txt`) is deleted, `rezepte.txt` will become a dangling link, meaning it will still exist but will no longer point to a valid target.

Question 84:

Imagine you have a flash drive plugged into your system, and mounted on /media/youruser/FlashA. You want to create a link called schematics.pdf in your home directory, pointing to the file esquema.pdf on the root of the flash drive. So, you type the command:

$ ln /media/youruser/FlashA/esquema.pdf ~/schematics.pdf

What would happen? Why?

A) A symbolic link will be created.

((**Correct**))

B) A hard link will be created.

C) The command will fail due to incorrect syntax.

D) A copy of the file will be created.

Explanation

The `ln` command without the `-s` option creates hard links by default. However, since the `-s` option is provided, it creates a symbolic link.

Question 85:

Consider the following output of ls -lah:

$ ls -lah

total 3,1M

drwxr-xr-x 2 carol carol 4,0K jun 17 17:27 .

drwxr-xr-x 5 carol carol 4,0K jun 17 17:29 ..

rw-rw-r-- 1 carol carol 2,8M jun 17 15:45 compressed.zip

rw-r--r-- 4 carol carol 77K jun 17 17:25 document.txt

rw-rw-r-- 1 carol carol 216K jun 17 17:25 image.png

rw-r--r-- 4 carol carol 77K jun 17 17:25 text.txt

How many links point to the file document.txt?

A) 1

B) 2

((**Correct**))

C) 3

D) 4

Explanation

The number of hard links is indicated by the number in the fourth column of the `ls` output. Here, `document.txt` has 4 links.

Question 86:

Are they soft or hard links?

A) Soft links

B) Hard links

((**Correct**))

Explanation

Hard links are indicated by the number in the fourth column of the `ls` output.

Question 87:

Which parameter should you pass to ls to see which inode each file occupies?

A) -i

((**Correct**))

B) -l

C) -n

D) -a

Explanation

The `-i` parameter with `ls` displays the inode number of each file.

Question 88:

Besides swap partitions, how can you quickly increase swap space on a Linux system?

A) By creating a new partition

B) By increasing the size of an existing partition

C) By creating a swap file

((**Correct**))

D) By resizing the root partition

Explanation

Besides swap partitions, swap space can be quickly increased on a Linux system by creating a swap file, which offers more flexibility compared to resizing partitions.

Question 89:

Someone just donated a laptop to your school and now you wish to install Linux on it. There is no manual and you were forced to boot it from a USB thumb drive with no graphics whatsoever. You do get a shell terminal and you know, for every processor you have there will be a line for it in the /proc/cpuinfo file: Using the commands grep and wc display how many processors you have.

A) `grep -c processor /proc/cpuinfo | wc -l`

((**Correct**))

B) `grep processor /proc/cpuinfo | wc -l`

C) `grep -c processor /proc/cpuinfo`

D) `grep processor /proc/cpuinfo | wc`

Explanation

This command will count the occurrences of the "processor" keyword in the /proc/cpuinfo file, which corresponds to the number of processors, and then pipe the output to `wc -l` to count the lines.

Question 90:

Consider a remote filesystem mounted at /mnt/server, which has become unreachable due to a loss of network connectivity. How could you force it to be unmounted, or mounted as readonly if this is not possible?

A) `umount -f /mnt/server`

B) `mount -o remount,ro /mnt/server`

C) `umount -l /mnt/server`

((**Correct**))

D) `mount -o force /mnt/server`

Explanation

The `-l` or `--lazy` option in `umount` attempts to unmount the filesystem immediately, but if it fails due to the filesystem being busy, it detaches the filesystem from the file hierarchy (lazy unmount), allowing administrators to address the underlying issue.

PRACTICE TEST FOUR - LPIC-1 EXAM 101 VERSION: 5.0

90 questions | 2 hours | 90% correct required to pass

The LPIC-1 Exam 101 Version: 5.0 Practice Test is a comprehensive resource designed to prepare you for the LPIC-1 (Linux Professional Institute Certification) Exam 101. It includes practice questions that mimic the format and content of the actual test. Each **Question** comes with a detailed **Explanation** to help you understand the concepts better. This practice test is an excellent tool to harness the power of Linux and achieve LPIC-1 certification.

Question 1:

What is the primary function of the udev subsystem in Linux?

A) To manage user accounts and permissions.

B) To block the loading of specific kernel modules.

C) To dynamically create corresponding device files in /dev.

((**Correct**))

D) To list all currently loaded kernel modules.

Explanation

The primary function of the udev subsystem in Linux is to dynamically create corresponding device files in /dev.

Question 2:

What command is used to display detailed information about a specific kernel module, including available parameters?

A) modprobe

B) lsmod

C) modinfo

((**Correct**))

D) insmod

Explanation

The modinfo command is used to display detailed information about a specific kernel module, including available parameters.

Question 3:

Which directory contains files with information regarding running processes and hardware resources in Linux?

A) /proc

((**Correct**))

B) /dev

C) /sys

D) /mnt

Explanation

The /proc directory contains files with information regarding running processes and hardware resources in Linux.

Question 4:

On a machine equipped with a BIOS firmware, where is the bootstrap binary located?

A) Master Boot Record (MBR)

((**Correct**))

B) EFI System Partition (ESP)

C) /boot directory

D) /etc directory

Explanation

The bootstrap binary, typically the first stage of the bootloader, is located in the Master Boot Record (MBR) on machines with BIOS firmware.

Question 5:

UEFI firmware supports extended features provided by external programs, called EFI applications. These applications, however, have their own special location. Where on the system would the EFI applications be located?

A) /boot directory

B) /etc directory

C) EFI System Partition (ESP)

((**Correct**))

D) /bin directory

Explanation

EFI applications are stored in the EFI System Partition (ESP), a special partition used by UEFI firmware to store boot loaders and other related files.

Question 6:

Bootloaders allow the passing of custom kernel parameters before loading it. Suppose the system is unable to boot due to a misinformed root filesystem location. How would the correct root filesystem, located at /dev/sda3, be given as a parameter to the kernel?

A) By modifying the /etc/fstab file

B) By editing the bootloader configuration file

((**Correct**))

C) By modifying the /etc/default/grub file

D) By running the mkinitrd command

Explanation

The correct root filesystem can be specified as a parameter to the kernel by editing the bootloader configuration file, such as GRUB configuration file, and adding `root=/dev/sda3` to the kernel command line.

Question 7:

How could the telinit command be used to reboot the system?

A) `telinit 6`

((**Correct**))

B) `telinit -r`

C) `telinit 0`

D) `telinit --reboot`

Explanation

In SysVinit systems, including Linux distributions like CentOS 6 and earlier, the `telinit` command can be used to change the system's runlevel. Runlevel 6 typically represents system reboot, so `telinit 6` would initiate a reboot.

Question 8:

Consider the command below:

$ cp /home/frank/emp_name /home/frank/backup

If emp_name was a directory what option should be added to cp to execute the command?

A) -d

B) -r

((**Correct**))

C) -p

D) -s

Explanation

The `-r` option is used with `cp` to recursively copy

directories and their contents.

Question 9:

Consider the command below:

$ cp /home/frank/emp_name /home/frank/backup

If cp is now changed to mv what results do you expect?

A) emp_name would be copied to /home/frank/backup.

B) emp_name would be deleted.

C) emp_name would be moved to /home/frank/backup.

((**Correct**))

D) emp_name would be renamed.

Explanation

The `mv` command moves the file emp_name to the directory /home/frank/backup.

Question 10:

Consider the listing:

$ ls file1.txt file2.txt file3.txt file4.txt

Which wildcard would help to delete all the contents of this directory?

A) *

((**Correct**))

B) ?

C)

D) []

Explanation

The * wildcard matches any string of characters, so using `rm *` would delete all files in the directory.

Question 11:

What will be the result of command `cat <<.>/dev/stdout`?

A) Prints nothing

((**Correct**))

B) Prints a dot (.)

C) Prints the contents of the current directory

D) Prints the contents of the file `/dev/stdout`

Explanation

This command uses a here document with a delimiter set to a dot (.), but since there's no input provided, it prints nothing.

Question 12:

The command `cat /proc/cpu_info` displays an error message because `/proc/cpu_info` is nonexistent. The command `cat /proc/cpu_info 2>1` redirects the error message to where?

A) STDOUT

((**Correct**))

B) STDERR

C) STDIN

D) /dev/null

Explanation

`2>1` redirects STDERR (standard error) to the file named `1`, which is then treated as STDOUT (standard output), essentially sending the error message to the terminal.

Question 13:

Will it still be possible to discard content sent to `/dev/null` if the noclobber option is enabled for the current shell session?

A) Yes

((**Correct**))

B) No

Explanation

The `noclobber` option does not affect redirection to `/dev/null`. `/dev/null` is a special file that discards all data written to it regardless of shell settings.

Question 14:

Without using `echo`, how could the contents of the variable `$USER` be redirected to the stdin of command `sha1sum`?

A) `sha1sum < $USER`

B) `$USER | sha1sum`

C) `sha1sum <<< $USER`

((**Correct**))

D) `sha1sum -i $USER`

Explanation

`<<<` is a here string that redirects the contents of `$USER` to the stdin of `sha1sum`.

Question 15:

Type the ps command to display all processes started by the Apache HTTPD web server user (www-data): Using BSD syntax:

A) ps -U www-data

B) ps -u www-data

((**Correct**))

C) ps -w www-data

D) ps -l www-data

Explanation

The correct answer is B) ps -u www-data.

Option B) provides the correct command to display all processes started by the Apache HTTPD web server user (www-data) using BSD syntax. Let's delve into the explanation:

ps: This command is used to display information about active processes.

-u www-data: This option specifies that ps should display processes owned by the user www-data.

Combining these options (ps -u www-data) allows us to list all processes started by the Apache HTTPD web server user (www-data) using BSD syntax.

Now, let's briefly discuss the other options:

ps -U www-data: This option is incorrect because the -U option in BSD syntax is used to display processes owned by a user specified by their user ID, not their username.

ps -w www-data: This option is incorrect because the -w option is used in BSD syntax to indicate wide output, but it is not relevant for filtering processes by user.

ps -l www-data: This option is incorrect because the -l option in BSD syntax is used to display a long listing format, which includes additional information about processes such as the process ID, terminal associated with the process, CPU usage, etc. It does not filter processes by user.

Therefore, option B) ps -u www-data is the correct choice as it represents the command that effectively displays all processes started by the Apache HTTPD web server user (www-data) using BSD syntax.

Question 16:

Type the ps command to display all processes started by the Apache HTTPD web server user (www-data): Using UNIX syntax:

A) ps -u www-data

((**Correct**))

B) ps -U www-data

C) ps -w www-data

D) ps -l www-data

Explanation

The correct answer is A) ps -u www-data.

Option A) provides the correct command to display all

processes started by the Apache HTTPD web server user (www-data) using UNIX syntax. Let's delve into the explanation:

ps: This command is used to display information about active processes.

-u www-data: This option specifies that ps should display processes owned by the user www-data.

Combining these options (ps -u www-data) allows us to list all processes started by the Apache HTTPD web server user (www-data) using UNIX syntax.

Now, let's briefly discuss the other options:

B) ps -U www-data: This option is incorrect because the -U option in UNIX syntax is used to display processes with a specified user ID, not their username.

ps -w www-data: This option is incorrect because the -w option is used in UNIX syntax to indicate wide output, but it is not relevant for filtering processes by user.

ps -l www-data: This option is incorrect because the -l option in UNIX syntax is used to display a long listing format, which includes additional information about processes such as the process ID, terminal associated with the process, CPU usage, etc. It does not filter processes by user.

Therefore, option A) ps -u www-data is the correct choice as it represents the command that effectively displays all processes started by the Apache HTTPD web server user (www-data) using UNIX syntax.

Question 17:

Scenario:

You want to list all processes currently running on your system that were started by the Apache web server user (typically www-data).

Question: Which ps command displays all processes owned by the user www-data using UNIX syntax?

A) `ps -U www-data`

B) `ps -u www-data`

((**Correct**))

C) `ps -w www-data`

D) `ps -l www-data`

Explanation

Answer: (A) ps -u www-data

The ps command displays information about running processes. The options used here are:

-u**: This flag allows filtering processes by the effective user ID (UID).

www-data**: This is the user account typically used by the Apache web server on many Linux systems.

Breakdown of other options:

B) ps -U www-data: This option uses the process User ID (PID) instead of the user name. While filtering by PID is possible, using the user name is generally more convenient.

C) ps -w www-data: The -w flag is used for wide output format, not user filtering.

D) ps -l www-data: The -l flag provides a long format with detailed process information, but it doesn't filter by user.

Question 18:

The SIGHUP signal can be used as a way to restart certain daemons. With the Apache HTTPD web server — for example — sending SIGHUP to the parent process (the one started by init) kills off its children. The parent, however, re-reads its configuration files, re-opens log files, and spawns a new set of children. Do the following tasks:

Start the web server:

A) sudo service apache2 start

B) systemctl start apache2

((**Correct**))

C) sudo /etc/init.d/apache2 start

D) apache2ctl start

Explanation

The correct answer is B) systemctl start apache2.

Option B) systemctl start apache2 is the correct command to start the Apache HTTPD web server using systemctl, which is the preferred method in modern Linux distributions. Let's delve into the explanation:

systemctl: This command is a central management tool for controlling systemd services, including starting, stopping, enabling, and disabling services.

start apache2: This option instructs systemctl to start the apache2 service.

Combining these options (systemctl start apache2) allows us to start the Apache HTTPD web server using the systemd service manager, ensuring proper initialization and management of the service.

Now, let's briefly discuss the other options:

sudo service apache2 start: This option uses the legacy service command to start the apache2 service. While this command may work on some systems, it is not the recommended approach in modern Linux distributions using systemd.

sudo /etc/init.d/apache2 start: This option directly executes the apache2 init script located in /etc/init.d/. While this may start the Apache HTTPD web server on some systems, it bypasses the service manager and is not the preferred method.

apache2ctl start: This option uses the apache2ctl command-line utility to start the Apache HTTPD web server. While this command may work, it is less commonly used compared to systemctl for managing services in modern Linux distributions.

Therefore, option B) systemctl start apache2 is the correct choice as it represents the preferred and standard method to start the Apache HTTPD web server using systemctl in modern Linux distributions.

Question 19:

Scenario:

You need to determine the parent process ID (PPID) of the Apache web server process (often named apache2).

Question: Which command will effectively display the parent process ID (PPID) of the apache2 process?

A) `ps aux | grep apache2`

B) `pgrep apache2`

C) `pidof apache2`

((**Correct**))

D) `top`

Explanation

Here's a breakdown of the options and why they are not ideal for finding the PPID:

A) ps aux | grep apache2: This command can list all processes (ps aux) and filter for apache2, but it displays various information about the process, including the PID, but not necessarily the PPID.

B) pgrep apache2: This command outputs the PID (Process ID) of the first matching process named apache2. While useful for finding the main apache2 process, it doesn't directly show the PPID.

D) top: The top command displays a dynamic view of running processes, including PIDs. However, it doesn't explicitly show the PPID by default. You might need to configure additional options to view parent process information.

Using pidof for PPID (indirectly)

The pidof command is designed to find the process ID (PID) of the first matching process name. However, in most systems, it can be used to achieve the desired outcome here:

Running pidof apache2 returns the PID of the main apache2 process.

You can then use another ps command to get details about that specific process, including its PPID. For example, ps -o ppid= $(pidof apache2) will show the PPID of the apache2 process whose PID was retrieved by pidof.

Alternative with ps (more commands):

Use ps aux | grep apache2 to find the PID of an apache2 process.

Extract the PID (the first number) from the output.

Use ps -o ppid= <PID> (replace <PID> with the extracted PID) to find the PPID of that specific process.

While both methods achieve the goal, pidof is generally a more concise approach for this specific task.

Question 20:

Scenario:

You want to restart the Apache web server process gracefully.

Question: Which command correctly sends the SIGHUP signal to the parent process of the Apache web server to initiate a graceful restart?

A) kill -HUP <PID>

(**(Correct)**)

B) kill -SIGHUP <PID>

C) kill -1 <PID>

D) pkill -HUP apache2

Explanation

Here's a breakdown of the options and why they are incorrect:

B) kill -SIGHUP <PID>: While the syntax is mostly correct, using uppercase -HUP is the standard way to specify the signal.

C) kill -1 <PID>: The signal number 1 refers to SIGHUP, but it's better practice to use the symbolic name (HUP) for clarity and avoiding potential mistakes.

D) pkill -HUP apache2: While pkill can send signals to processes by name, it terminates all matching processes by default. This might not be desirable if you have multiple apache2 instances. Using kill with the PID ensures you target the specific parent process.

Recommended Approach:

Find the PID: Use pidof apache2 or ps aux | grep apache2 to identify the PID of the main apache2 process.

Restart with kill: Execute kill -HUP <PID> (replace <PID> with the actual PID). This sends the SIGHUP signal to the parent process, triggering a graceful restart where existing connections are gracefully terminated before starting new ones.

Note: It's generally advisable to use a service management tool like systemctl (for systemd) or service (for SysV init) to restart Apache for proper integration with the system's service management framework. This approach might also handle dependencies and logging more effectively.

Question 21:

Scenario:

You restarted the Apache web server using kill -HUP <PID> (where <PID> is the parent process ID). Now, you want to confirm the restart was successful.

Question: Which command effectively verifies that the parent process of the Apache web server is still running and has spawned new child processes?

A) ps aux | grep apache2

((**Correct**))

B) pgrep apache2

C) pidof apache2

D) top

Explanation

Here's a breakdown of the options and why they might not be ideal for this specific task:

B) pgrep apache2: This outputs the PID of the first matching apache2 process, but it doesn't tell you if the parent process is still alive or if new children have been spawned.

C) pidof apache2: Similar to pgrep, it finds the PID of the first apache2 process, lacking details about child processes.

D) top: While top displays a dynamic view of processes, it might require additional configuration to show the parent-child relationships clearly.

Using ps aux | grep apache2:

This command provides a more comprehensive view:

ps aux: This lists all processes with detailed information, including PIDs, user, and command name.

grep apache2: This filters the output to show only processes containing "apache2" in the command name.

By examining the output, you can see:

If there's an apache2 process with the same PID as before the restart, the parent process is likely still running.

If there are multiple apache2 processes with different PIDs compared to before, it suggests new child processes have been spawned.

Alternative with ps (more specific):

Use pidof apache2 to get the PID before the restart (store it as <old_pid>).

Run ps -o pid,ppid= $(pidof apache2) to get the PID and parent PID of the current main apache2 process.

Compare the current PID with <old_pid>. If they differ, the parent process restarted.

Look for additional apache2 processes in the output besides the main one. This suggests new child processes were spawned.

Question 22:

Scenario:

You want to monitor the Apache web server for new connections in real-time. Before proceeding, it's important to understand the MaxConnectionsPerChild directive in Apache configuration.

Understanding MaxConnectionsPerChild

The MaxConnectionsPerChild directive within the Apache configuration limits the number of concurrent connections a single child process can handle. Setting it to 1 ensures each child process manages only one connection at a time. This can be useful for monitoring purposes (as in this question) but might not be ideal for real-world scenarios due to potential performance overhead.

Question: Which directive sets the maximum number of connections per child process in the Apache configuration file?

A) MaxConnectionsPerChild 1

((**Correct**))

B) MaxClientsPerChild 1

C) MaxRequestsPerChild 1

D) MaxProcessesPerChild 1

Explanation

Answer: (A) MaxConnectionsPerChild 1

The other options are incorrect because they represent different directives:

B) MaxClientsPerChild: This directive (not commonly used) defines the maximum number of requests a child process can handle before being restarted.

C) MaxRequestsPerChild: This directive sets the maximum number of requests a child process can serve before being restarted.

D) MaxProcessesPerChild: This directive (likely a typo) doesn't exist in Apache configuration. The correct term is MaxClients or MaxSpareServers, which define the total number of child processes to spawn.

Monitoring with ps and watch (Not included in the original question)

While modifying MaxConnectionsPerChild can be helpful for monitoring, it's not recommended for production due to performance reasons. Here's how to monitor new connections dynamically using ps and watch:

Run watch ps -ef | grep httpd (or watch ps -ef | grep apache2) in your terminal. This continuously executes ps with the -ef flag (showing all processes) and filters output containing "httpd" or "apache2" (depending on your system).

Important Note: Modifying MaxConnectionsPerChild to 1 is intended for demonstration purposes only. It's not suitable for a typical production environment.

Question 23:

Type in a command that uses watch, ps, and grep for apache2 connections.

A) watch "ps aux | grep apache2"

B) watch "ps -ef | grep apache2"

((**Correct**))

C) watch "ps -aux | grep apache2"

D) watch "ps -e | grep apache2"

Explanation

The correct answer is B) watch "ps -ef | grep apache2".

Option B) provides the correct command to use watch, ps, and grep for monitoring Apache HTTPD connections. Let's delve into the explanation:

watch: This command is used to execute a command repeatedly and display its output in real-time.

ps -ef: This command lists all processes in a full-format listing, allowing us to see detailed information about each process, including the command line used to start it.

grep apache2: This command filters the output of ps to only show lines containing "apache2", effectively showing only the Apache HTTPD processes.

Combining these commands with watch (watch "ps -ef | grep apache2") allows us to continuously monitor Apache HTTPD connections in real-time by updating the ps output every 2 seconds by default (unless specified otherwise).

Now, let's briefly discuss the other options:

watch "ps aux | grep apache2": This option is incorrect because it uses the aux option with ps, which is not compatible with the way grep filters the output. The -ef option is preferred for compatibility across different Unix-like systems.

watch "ps -aux | grep apache2": This option is incorrect because it combines the aux option with ps without a leading hyphen, resulting in an invalid command. Additionally, it is recommended to use -ef instead of aux for compatibility.

watch "ps -e | grep apache2": This option is incorrect because it only lists all processes (ps -e), which may not provide detailed information about Apache HTTPD processes. Additionally, it does not use the -f option to provide a full-format listing of processes.

Therefore, option B) watch "ps -ef | grep apache2" is the correct choice as it represents the command that effectively uses watch, ps, and grep for monitoring Apache HTTPD connections.

Question 24:

Scenario:

You've restarted the Apache web server using kill -HUP <PID> and verified its successful restart with ps aux | grep apache2. Now, you'll access the server using a web browser.

Question: Assuming watch ps -ef | grep httpd (or watch ps -ef | grep apache2) is running, what do you expect to see in the output after establishing a connection to the web server through its IP address?

A) Continuously updating list of apache2 processes.

((**Correct**))

B) Blank screen.

C) Error message.

D) Static list of processes.

Explanation

Answer: (A) Continuously updating list of apache2 processes.

Here's why the other options are incorrect:

B) Blank screen: The watch command continues running the ps command periodically, so it shouldn't go completely blank.

C) Error message: Unless there's an unexpected issue with ps, you shouldn't encounter an error message due to a web browser request.

D) Static list of processes: The key aspect of watch is that it executes the command repeatedly. After establishing a web browser connection, the ps command within watch should show an updated list with potentially more child processes under the apache2 parent process (depending on your configuration). This indicates new child processes were spawned to handle the incoming request.

What you might see:

You might see the existing apache2 process remain with the same PID, but additional child processes with different PIDs might appear in the list.

The number of child processes can fluctuate depending on server configuration and connection handling.

Note: The specific output format and details displayed by ps might vary depending on your system. However, the general idea is that you should observe a dynamic update in the process list after accessing the web server.

Question 25:

Scenario:

By default, top sorts processes by CPU usage. You want to view them sorted by memory usage instead.

Question: Which command launches top with the processes sorted by memory usage?

A) top -o %MEM

(**(Correct)**)

B) top -o mem

C) top -o %MEM -O mem

D) top -o mem -O %MEM

Explanation

Answer: (A) top -o %MEM

Here's a breakdown of the options and why they are incorrect:

B) top -o mem: While "mem" might seem intuitive, the correct option for memory usage is %MEM.

C) top -o %MEM -O mem: Using multiple -o flags is not recommended. The first encountered -o option with a valid sorting field will be applied. Here, %MEM takes precedence.

D) top -o mem -O %MEM: Similar to option C, the order of -o flags matters. Here, mem would be ignored, and the default

CPU sorting would be used.

Sorting with top -o %MEM:

top: This launches the top command.

-o %MEM: This option specifies the sorting field. %MEM indicates sorting by the percentage of memory used by each process.

Running this command displays the top utility with processes sorted by their memory usage, with the highest memory consumers at the top.

Question 26:

Scenario:

You're using the top command to monitor processes. You want to quickly sort the displayed processes by their memory usage.

Question: Which keyboard shortcut in top highlights the memory column and sorts the processes by memory usage (descending order)?

A) Press Shift + M

((**Correct**))

B) Press Shift + H

C) Press Shift + F

D) Press Shift + P

Explanation

Answer: (A) Press Shift + M

top provides interactive features accessible through keyboard shortcuts. Here's what each option does:

A) Press Shift + M: This is the correct shortcut. Pressing Shift and M together highlights the "%MEM" (memory usage) column and sorts the processes according to their memory consumption, with the highest memory users at the top.

B) Press Shift + H: There's no standard shortcut Shift + H in top.

C) Press Shift + F: Pressing Shift + F opens the interactive menu for selecting sorting criteria. You can then use arrow keys and Enter to choose "%MEM" for sorting by memory.

D) Press Shift + P: Pressing Shift and P together highlights the "%CPU" (CPU usage) column and sorts the processes by CPU consumption.

Using Shift + M is the most efficient way to sort by memory usage without needing to navigate menus.

Question 27:

Scenario:

You want to see a specific set of details about running processes: user, memory usage, CPU usage, and the full command line for each process.

Question: Which command displays information about user, memory usage, CPU usage, and the full command for each process using ps?

A) ps -o user,%mem,%cpu,cmd

((**Correct**))

B) ps -eo user,%mem,%cpu,cmd

C) ps -o user,pmem,pcpu,cmd

D) ps -eo user,pmem,pcpu,cmd

Explanation

Answer: (A) ps -o user,%mem,%cpu,cmd

Here's a breakdown of the options and why they might not be ideal:

B) ps -eo user,%mem,%cpu,cmd: While the -e flag is optional for all processes (the default), it doesn't affect the output format. Option (A) is more concise.

C) ps -o user,pmem,pcpu,cmd: These options use incorrect abbreviations for memory and CPU usage. The correct options are %mem and %cpu.

D) ps -eo user,pmem,pcpu,cmd: Similar to option (C), it uses incorrect abbreviations for memory and CPU usage.

Using ps -o user,%mem,%cpu,cmd:

ps: This launches the ps command to display process information.

-o user,%mem,%cpu,cmd:

-o: This option specifies the output format.

user: This displays the username of the process owner.

%mem: This displays the percentage of memory used by the process.

%cpu: This displays the percentage of CPU time used by the process.

cmd: This displays the full command line used to launch the process.

This command provides a focused view of processes including their owners, resource usage, and the complete commands that started them.

Question 28:

Scenario:

You want to see a concise view of running processes, showing only the user who owns the process and the name of the program being executed.

Question: Which ps command displays user names and program names for running processes?

A) ps -o user,cmd

((**Correct**))

B) ps -e

C) ps -eo user

D) ps -o user

Explanation

Answer: (A) ps -o user,cmd

Here's a breakdown of the options and why they might not be ideal:

B) ps -e: This flag tells ps to list all processes, but it doesn't control the output format. You'd need to combine it with -o for specific columns.

C) ps -eo user: This option only shows the user for each process, omitting the program name.

D) ps -o user: Similar to option (C), it only shows the user for each process.

Using ps -o user,cmd:

ps: This launches the ps command to display process information.

-o user,cmd:

-o: This option specifies the output format.

user: This displays the username of the process owner.

cmd: This displays the name of the program being executed (though it might be truncated by default).

This command provides a compact view listing the user and the program name (command name) for each running process.

Question 29:

What is the purpose of a terminal multiplexer like GNU Screen or tmux?

A) To emulate multiple independent terminals on a single physical terminal

(**(Correct)**)

B) To enhance the graphical user interface of Linux systems

C) To create virtual desktops for multitasking

D) To replace the default shell with a more efficient one

Explanation

Terminal multiplexers allow users to manage multiple terminal sessions within a single window, enhancing productivity by enabling multitasking and efficient use of system resources.

Question 30:

How can the priority of all processes owned by a specific user be modified in Linux?

A) Using the renice command with the -g option

B) Using the renice command with the -u option

((**Correct**))

C) Using the top command with the r option

D) Using the nice command with the -n option

Explanation

The renice command in Linux allows the priority of all processes owned by a specific user to be modified using the -u option.

Question 31:

Which command can be used to display detailed process information and sort processes based on CPU usage?

A) ps -el

((**Correct**))

B) top

C) nice

D) renice

Explanation

The ps command with the -el option displays detailed process information and can sort processes based on CPU usage, providing insights into process priorities.

Question 32:

What is the purpose of the Linux scheduler in a multi-processing environment?

A) To ensure only one process controls the CPU at a time

B) To organize the process queue and decide which process to execute

((**Correct**))

C) To assign a unique priority to each process

D) To prevent processes from making system calls indefinitely

Explanation

The Linux scheduler organizes the process queue in a multi-processing environment, determining which process to execute next based on priorities and other factors.

Question 33:

What extended regular expression would only match any IPv4 address in the standard dotted-quad format, like 192.168.15.1?

A) `^(\d{1,3}\.){3}\d{1,3}$`

B) `^(\d{1,3}\.){4}$`

C) `^\d{1,3}\.\d{1,3}\.\d{1,3}\.\d{1,3}$`

((**Correct**))

D) `^(\d{1,3}\.){2}\d{1,3}$`

Explanation

This regular expression matches IPv4 addresses in the dotted-quad format, where each segment consists of 1 to 3 digits separated by dots.

Question 34:

How can the grep command be used to list the contents of file /etc/services, discarding all comments (lines starting with #)?

A) `grep -v "^#" /etc/services`

((**Correct**))

B) `grep -e "^[^#]+" /etc/services`

C) `grep -v "^[#].*" /etc/services`

D) `grep -e "^[^#].*" /etc/services`

Explanation

The `-v` option in grep inverts the match, so lines starting with `#` are discarded, effectively removing comments from the output.

Question 35:

The file domains.txt contains a list of domain names, one per line. How would the egrep command be used to list only .org or .com domains?

A) `egrep '\.org$|\.com$' domains.txt`

((**Correct**))

B) `egrep '*.org$|*.com$' domains.txt`

C) `egrep '\.org\|.com' domains.txt`

D) `egrep 'org$|com$' domains.txt`

Explanation

This egrep command uses a regular expression to match lines ending with either `.org` or `.com`, filtering out other domain extensions.

Question 36:

From the current directory, how would the find command use an extended regular expression to search for all files not containing a standard file suffix (file names not ending in .txt or .c, for example)?

A) `find . -type f ! -regex '.*\(\.txt\|\.c\)$'`

((**Correct**))

B) `find . -type f -regex '!.*\(\.txt\|\.c\)$'`

C) `find . -type f ! -name '*.txt' ! -name '*.c'`

D) `find . -type f -regex '\(\.txt\|\.c\)$' -not`

Explanation

This find command searches for all files (`-type f`) in the current directory and subdirectories that do not match the given regular expression, which excludes files ending with `.txt` or `.c`.

Question 37:

Which command is used to change the default text editor in the shell environment?

A) export EDITOR=vi

((**Correct**))

B) export EDITOR=nano

C) export EDITOR=emacs

D) export EDITOR=vim

Explanation

The `export EDITOR=editor_name` command is used to change the default text editor in the shell environment. In this case, `vi` is being set as the default editor.

Question 38:

What key in vi is used to navigate to the end of the document?

A) $

B) G

((**Correct**))

C) gg

D) %

Explanation

In vi, pressing the `G` key in Normal mode navigates the cursor to the end of the document.

Question 39:

Which editor is known as a modern replacement for vi and offers features such as syntax highlighting and multi-level undo/redo?

A) nano

B) Emacs

C) vim

((**Correct**))

D) sed

Explanation

Vim (Vi IMproved) is known as a modern replacement for vi, offering enhancements such as syntax highlighting, multi-level undo/redo, and multi-document editing.

Question 40:

Using parted, what is the command to create a 300 MB ext4 partition, starting at 500 MB on the disk?

A) `mkpart primary 500M 300M ext4`

B) `mkpart primary ext4 500M 300M`

C) `mkpart primary ext4 300M 500M`

D) `mkpart primary 300M 500M ext4`

((**Correct**))

Explanation

The command `mkpart primary 300M 500M ext4` creates a primary partition starting at 300 MB and ending at 500 MB, formatted with the ext4 filesystem.

Question 41:

What will happen to the services related to the file /etc/rc1.d/K90network when the system enters runlevel 1?

A) They will be started.

B) They will be stopped.

((**Correct**))

C) They will be restarted.

D) They will remain unaffected.

Explanation

In the SysVinit system, the `K` prefix in the `/etc/rc1.d` directory indicates scripts to stop services when transitioning to runlevel 1. Therefore, the services related to `/etc/rc1.d/K90network` will be stopped when entering runlevel 1.

Question 42:

Using command systemctl, how could a user verify if the unit sshd.service is running?

A) `systemctl check sshd.service`

B) `systemctl status sshd.service`

((**Correct**))

C) `systemctl verify sshd.service`

D) `systemctl show sshd.service`

Explanation

The `systemctl status` command is used to display the status of a systemd unit. Therefore, `systemctl status sshd.service` would provide information about whether the `sshd.service` unit is running or not.

Question 43:

On Linux systems, where are the files for the GRUB bootloader stored?

A) /boot/grub

((**Correct**))

B) /etc/grub

C) /boot/loader

D) /boot/config

Explanation

The GRUB bootloader files are typically stored in the `/boot/grub` directory on Linux systems.

Question 44:

Where should the boot partition end to ensure that a PC will always be able to load the kernel?

A) Before the 1024th cylinder

((**Correct**))

B) After the 1024th sector

C) At the end of the disk

D) Before the 1024th sector

Explanation

To ensure compatibility with older BIOS systems, the boot partition should end before the 1024th cylinder of the disk.

Question 45:

Where is the EFI partition usually mounted?

A) /efi

B) /boot/efi

((**Correct**))

C) /boot/efi/EFI

D) /boot

Explanation

The EFI partition is usually mounted at `/boot/efi` in Linux systems using the EFI (Extensible Firmware Interface) boot method.

Question 46:

What is the default location for the GRUB 2 configuration file?

A) /etc/grub2.cfg

B) /boot/grub/grub.cfg

((**Correct**))

C) /boot/grub2/grub.cfg

D) /etc/default/grub

Explanation

The default location for the GRUB 2 configuration file is `/boot/grub/grub.cfg`.

Question 47:

What are the steps needed to change the settings for GRUB 2?

A) Edit the configuration file and run update-grub

((**Correct**))

B) Run grub-install with the new settings

C) Modify the kernel parameters directly from the boot menu

D) Reboot the system and select the desired settings

Explanation

To change the settings for GRUB 2, you need to edit the configuration file (typically `/etc/default/grub` or `/etc/grub.d/`) and then run `update-grub` to apply the changes.

Question 48:

Into which file should custom GRUB 2 menu entries be added?

A) /boot/grub/custom.cfg

B) /etc/grub.d/40_custom

((**Correct**))

C) /etc/grub2/custom.cfg

D) /boot/grub/grub.cfg

Explanation

Custom GRUB 2 menu entries should be added to the file `/etc/grub.d/40_custom`.

Question 49:

Where are the menu entries for GRUB Legacy stored?

A) /boot/grub/menu.lst

((**Correct**))

B) /etc/grub/menu.lst

C) /boot/grub/grub.cfg

D) /etc/grub2/grub.cfg

Explanation

The menu entries for GRUB Legacy are stored in the file `/boot/grub/menu.lst`.

Question 50:

Which environment variable is used to specify additional paths for shared libraries temporarily in a Linux system?

A) LIBRARY_PATH

B) SHARED_LIB_PATH

C) LD_PATH

D) LD_LIBRARY_PATH

((**Correct**))

Explanation

The correct answer is D) The LD_LIBRARY_PATH environment variable is used to specify additional paths for shared libraries temporarily in a Linux system.

Question 51:

What information does the ldd command provide when used with the -u option?

A) Unused direct dependencies

((**Correct**))

B) Used direct dependencies

C) Unused indirect dependencies

D) Used indirect dependencies

Explanation

The correct answer is A) The ldd command with the -u option prints the unused direct dependencies of a program.

Question 52:

You have developed a piece of software and want to add a new shared library directory to your system (/opt/lib/mylib). You write its absolute path in a file called mylib.conf. In what directory should you put this file?

A) /etc/ld.so.conf.d

((**Correct**))

B) /usr/lib

C) /opt/lib

D) /usr/local/lib

Explanation

Configuration files for the dynamic linker/loader are placed in the directory `/etc/ld.so.conf.d`.

Question 53:

What is the purpose of the /etc/apt/sources.list file?

A) To list installed packages

B) To list the contents of a package

C) To specify package repositories

((**Correct)**)

D) To store package configuration files

Explanation

The /etc/apt/sources.list file is used to specify package repositories from which packages can be downloaded and installed.

Question 54:

Which command is used to reconfigure an installed package?

A) dpkg-reconfigure

((**Correct)**)

B) apt-get update

C) apt-get install

D) apt-get remove

Explanation

The dpkg-reconfigure utility is used to reconfigure an installed package.

Question 55:

What is the purpose of the "apt-get clean" command?

A) To remove unused dependencies

B) To update the package index

C) To remove cached package files

((**Correct**))

D) To list installed packages

Explanation

The "clean" parameter is used with apt-get to remove cached package files from the system.

Question 56:

Using rpm on a Red Hat Enterprise Linux system, how would you install the package fileroller-3.28.1-2.el7.x86_64.rpm showing a progress bar during the installation?

A) rpm -ivh --progress fileroller-3.28.1-2.el7.x86_64.rpm

((**Correct**))

B) rpm -Uvh --progress fileroller-3.28.1-2.el7.x86_64.rpm

C) rpm -Fvh --progress fileroller-3.28.1-2.el7.x86_64.rpm

D) rpm -qvh --progress fileroller-3.28.1-2.el7.x86_64.rpm

Explanation

The `-i` option installs the package, `-v` displays verbose output, and `-h` shows the progress bar during installation.

Question 57:

Using rpm, find out which package contains the file /etc/redhat-release.

A) rpm -qf /etc/redhat-release

((**Correct**))

B) rpm -Ql /etc/redhat-release

C) rpm -ql /etc/redhat-release

D) rpm -Qp /etc/redhat-release

Explanation

The `-qf` option in rpm is used to query which package owns a specific file.

Question 58:

How would you use yum to check for updates for all packages in the system?

A) yum check-update

((**Correct**))

B) yum update

C) yum list updates

D) yum upgrade

Explanation

The `yum check-update` command checks for updates for all packages in the system without performing the actual update.

Question 59:

Which command is used to generate a public and private SSH key pair?

A) ssh-copy-id

B) ssh-genkey

C) ssh-keygen

((**Correct**))

D) ssh-createkey

Explanation

ssh-keygen is used to generate a public and private SSH key pair for authentication.

Question 60:

What is the primary role of a hypervisor in virtualization?

A) To provide a virtualized environment for applications to run independently.

B) To manage physical hardware resources and allocate them to virtual machines.

((**Correct**))

C) To provide secure access to virtual machines over the internet.

D) To monitor system performance and resource usage of virtual machines.

Explanation

B) The primary role of a hypervisor is to manage physical hardware resources and allocate them to virtual machines.

Question 61:

Which command is used to print the contents of the `.bash_history` file in Linux?

A) `history`

B) `cat .bash_history`

((**Correct**))

C) `echo .bash_history`

D) `ls .bash_history`

Explanation

The correct answer is B) `cat .bash_history`. The `cat` command is used to concatenate and display the contents of files.

Question 62:

What is the purpose of using `grep` in conjunction with the `history` command?

A) To delete specific commands from history

B) To search for commands containing specific text in history

((**Correct**))

C) To append new commands to history

D) To list only the most recent commands in history

Explanation

The correct answer is B) To search for commands containing specific text in history. `grep` filters the output of the `history` command based on specified criteria.

Question 63:

How can you execute a previously run command without retyping it in Linux?

A) By using the `recall` command

B) By pressing the up arrow key

((**Correct**))

C) By typing `exec` followed by the command number

D) By using the `run` command followed by the command number

Explanation

The correct answer is B) By pressing the up arrow key. Pressing the up arrow key in the terminal allows you to cycle through previously executed commands for easy re-execution.

Question 64:

What is the purpose of the `wc` command in Linux?

A) To count the number of characters, words, and lines in a file.

((**Correct**))

B) To sort the lines of a file alphabetically.

C) To display the contents of a file.

D) To remove duplicate lines from a file.

Explanation

The correct answer is A) The `wc` command is used to count the number of characters, words, and lines in a file.

Question 65:

Which command is used to split larger files into smaller ones?

A) `split`

((**Correct**))

B) `cut`

C) `paste`

D) `tr`

Explanation

The correct answer is A) The `split` command is used to split larger files into smaller ones based on specified criteria.

Question 66:

Consider the command below:

$ cp /home/frank/emp_name /home/frank/backup

What would happen to the file emp_name if this command is executed successfully?

A) It would be moved to /home/frank/backup.

B) It would be copied to /home/frank/backup.

(**(Correct)**)

C) It would be deleted.

D) It would be renamed.

Explanation

The `cp` command copies the file emp_name to the directory /home/frank/backup.

Question 67:

Imagine you have 2 partitions, one on /dev/sda1 and the other on /dev/sda2, both 20 GB in size. How can you use them on a single Btrfs filesystem, in such a way that the contents of one partition will be automatically mirrored on the other, like on a RAID1 setup? How big will the filesystem be?

A) Create a RAID1 volume with both partitions; the filesystem will be 20 GB.

B) Create a RAIDO volume with both partitions; the filesystem will be 40 GB.

((**Correct**))

C) Create a Btrfs filesystem on one partition and use the other as a backup; the filesystem will be 20 GB.

D) Create a RAID1 volume with both partitions; the filesystem will be 20 GB.

Explanation

Creating a RAIDO volume (striped) combines the storage of both partitions, resulting in a 40 GB filesystem. RAID1 (mirrored) would provide redundancy but wouldn't double the storage capacity.

Question 68:

Consider a 2 GB disk with an MBR partition table and the following layout: Disk /dev/sdb: 1.9 GiB, 1998631936 bytes, 3903578 sectors. Can you create a 600 MB partition on it? Why?

A) Yes, because there is enough space available.

B) No, because the disk is too small.

C) No, because the existing partitions already occupy all available space.

((**Correct**))

D) Yes, because the MBR partition table supports large partitions.

Explanation

The existing partitions already consume the entire disk space, so there is no space available to create a new 600 MB partition.

Question 69:

On a disk at /dev/sdc, we have a first partition of 1 GB, containing about 256 MB of files. Using parted, how can you shrink it so it has just enough space for the files?

A) Resize the partition to 256 MB.

B) Resize the partition to 1 GB.

C) Resize the filesystem to 256 MB, then resize the partition to match.

((**Correct**))

D) You cannot shrink a partition.

Explanation

First, shrink the filesystem to 256 MB to match the amount of data. Then, resize the partition to match the new size of the filesystem.

Question 70:

Imagine you have a disk at /dev/sdb, and you want to create a 1 GB swap partition at the start of it. So, using parted, you create the partition with `mkpart primary linux-swap 0 1024M`. Then, you enable swap on this partition with `swapon /dev/sdb1`, but get the following error message: `swapon: /dev/sdb1: read swap header failed`. What went wrong?

A) The partition was not formatted.

((**Correct**))

B) The swap partition was not activated.

C) The partition size was too small.

D) The swap partition was already in use.

Explanation

The error indicates that the swap header could not be read, likely because the partition was not formatted as a swap partition using `mkswap`.

Question 71:

Using du, how can we check how much space is being used by just the files on the current directory?

A) `du -a`

B) `du -s`

((**Correct**))

C) `du -c`

D) `du -d 0`

Explanation

The `-s` option in the `du` command stands for "summarize," and it displays only the total size of the specified directories or files, without listing individual files.

Question 72:

Using df, list information for every ext4 filesystem, with the outputs including the following fields, in order: device, mount point, total number of inodes, number of available inodes, percentage of free space.

A) ` df -t ext4 -i `

B) ` df -T ext4 -i `

C) ` df -t ext4 -i -h `

D) ` df -T ext4 -i -h `

((**Correct**))

Explanation

The ` -T ` option specifies the filesystem type, ` -i ` displays inode-related information, and ` -h ` provides human-readable output.

Question 73:

What is the command to run e2fsck on /dev/sdc1 in non-interactive mode, while trying to automatically fix most errors?

A) ` e2fsck -p /dev/sdc1 `

B) ` e2fsck -y /dev/sdc1 `

((**Correct**))

C) ` e2fsck -r /dev/sdc1 `

D) ` e2fsck -a /dev/sdc1 `

Explanation

The ` -y ` option automatically answers "yes" to all questions asked by e2fsck, making it non-interactive. It also tries to automatically fix any errors found.

Question 74:

Using mount, how can you mount an ext4 filesystem on /dev/sdc1 to /mnt/external as read-only, using the noatime and async options?

A) `mount -o ro,noatime,async /dev/sdc1 /mnt/external`

((**Correct**))

B) `mount -o rw,noatime,async /dev/sdc1 /mnt/external`

C) `mount -o ro,noatime,async /mnt/external /dev/sdc1`

D) `mount -o rw,noatime,async /mnt/external /dev/sdc1`

Explanation

The `-o` option is used to specify mount options. Here, `ro` stands for read-only, `noatime` disables access time updates, and `async` enables asynchronous I/O for performance.

Question 75:

When unmounting a filesystem at /dev/sdd2, you get the "target is busy" error message. How can you find out which files on the filesystem are open, and what processes opened them?

A) `fuser -m /dev/sdd2`

B) `lsof /dev/sdd2`

((**Correct**))

C) `fuser -v /dev/sdd2`

D) `lsof -t /dev/sdd2`

Explanation

The `lsof` command lists open files and the processes that opened them. By specifying the device `/dev/sdd2`, you can identify which processes are keeping the filesystem busy.

Question 76:

Consider the following entry in /etc/fstab: `/dev/sdb1 /data ext4 noatime,noauto,async`. Will this filesystem be mounted if the command `mount -a` is issued? Why?

A) Yes, because `noauto` is not specified.

B) No, because `noauto` prevents automatic mounting.

((**Correct**))

C) Yes, because `noatime` overrides `noauto`.

D) No, because `async` is not specified.

Explanation

The `noauto` option in `/etc/fstab` prevents automatic mounting. Therefore, the filesystem will not be mounted when `mount -a` is issued.

Question 77:

What command is used to query the default permissions mask for files and directories?

A) mask

B) umask

((**Correct**))

C) perms

D) defaultmask

Explanation

The `umask` command is used to query or set the default permissions mask for files and directories.

Question 78:

What is the octal value for read, write, and execute permissions for the owner, group, and others?

A) 777

B) 666

C) 555

D) 777

((**Correct**))

Explanation

7 corresponds to read, write, and execute permissions for the owner, group, and others.

Question 79:

Create a directory named emptydir using the command mkdir emptydir. Now, using ls, list the permissions for the directory emptydir.

A) drwxr-xr-x

((**Correct**))

B) drwxrwxrwx

C) drwx------

D) d---------

Explanation

The `mkdir` command creates a directory with default permissions of 755 (rwxr-xr-x), which allows the owner to read, write, and execute, while others can only read and execute.

Question 80:

Create an empty file named emptyfile with the command touch emptyfile. Now, using chmod in symbolic mode, add execute permissions for the owner of the file emptyfile, and remove write and execute permissions for everyone else. Do this using only one chmod command.

A) chmod u+x,go-wx emptyfile

((**Correct**))

B) chmod u+x,go-w emptyfile

C) chmod u+x,o-w emptyfile

D) chmod u+x,go-wx emptyfile

Explanation

This command adds execute permission for the owner (`u +x`) and removes write and execute permissions for group and others (`go-wx`) in symbolic mode.

Question 81:

What would the default permissions for a file be if the umask value is set to 027?

A) -rwxr-xr-x

B) -rw-r-----

((**Correct**))

C) -rwxr-x---

D) -rw-r-xr--

Explanation

The umask value subtracts from the default permissions. In this case, it removes write and execute permissions for group and others, leaving `-rw-r-----`.

Question 82:

Imagine you have in your ~/Documents directory a file named clients.txt containing some client names, and a directory named somedir. Inside this there is a different file also named clients.txt with different names. To replicate this structure, use the following commands.

$ cd ~/Documents

$ echo "John, Michael, Bob" > clients.txt

$ mkdir somedir

$ echo "Bill, Luke, Karl" > somedir/clients.txt

You then create a link inside somedir named partners.txt pointing to this file, with the commands:

$ cd somedir/

$ ln -s clients.txt partners.txt

So, the directory structure is:

Documents

|-- clients.txt

`-- somedir

|-- clients.txt

`-- partners.txt -> clients.txt

Now, you move partners.txt from somedir to ~/Documents, and list its contents.

$ cd ~/Documents/

$ mv somedir/partners.txt .

$ less partners.txt

Will the link still work? If so, which file will have its contents listed? Why?

A) Yes, `partners.txt` will still work and list the contents of `clients.txt` inside `somedir`.

B) No, the link will break because it's moved out of `somedir`.

C) Yes, `partners.txt` will still work and list the contents of `clients.txt` in `~/Documents`.

((**Correct**))

D) No, the link will break because it's moved to a different directory.

Explanation

Symbolic links store the path to their target file, so moving the symbolic link itself does not affect its functionality. The contents of `partners.txt` will still point to `clients.txt`, even though `partners.txt` has been moved to a different directory.

Question 83:

How is the size of a Logical Volume defined?

A) In kilobytes (KB)

B) In megabytes (MB)

C) In gigabytes (GB)

((**Correct**))

D) In percentage of the Volume Group size

Explanation

The size of a Logical Volume (LV) in LVM is typically defined in gigabytes (GB), but it can also be specified in other units like kilobytes (KB) or megabytes (MB).

Question 84:

Besides swap partitions, how can you quickly increase swap space on a Linux system?

A) Add a new physical disk

B) Create a swap file

((**Correct**))

C) Resize an existing partition

D) Increase the size of the existing swap partition

Explanation

Besides swap partitions, you can quickly increase swap space on a Linux system by creating a swap file using the `dd` and `mkswap` commands.

Question 85:

How can you get a list of all installed packages in the system using dnf?

A) dnf list installed

((**Correct**))

B) dnf list --installed

C) dnf installed

D) dnf show installed

Explanation

The `dnf list installed` command lists all installed packages in the system.

Question 86:

Use the apropos tool to identify the man page where you will find the command you will need to display the size of an attached physical block device in bytes rather than megabytes or gigabytes.

A) blkid

B) lsblk

((**Correct**))

C) fdisk

D) df

Explanation

The `lsblk` command can be used to display information about block devices, including their size, in bytes.

Question 87:

What command is used to display a file's contents in hexadecimal format?

A) `od`

((Correct))

B) `less`

C) `cat`

D) `tail`

Explanation

The correct answer is A) The `od` command displays a file's contents in octal, decimal, or hexadecimal format.

Question 88:

A user wishes to compress his backup folder. He uses the following command:

$ tar cvf /home/frank/backup.tar.gz /home/frank/dir1

Which option is lacking to compress the backup using the gzip algorithm?

A) -c

B) -v

C) -f

D) -z

((Correct))

Explanation

The `-z` option is used with `tar` to compress the archive using gzip. Without this option, the archive is not compressed.

Question 89:

How could the output of command `date +%Y-%m-%d` be used as a Here string to command `sed s/-/./g`?

A) `sed s/-/./g <<< $(date +%Y-%m-%d)`

((**Correct**))

B) `sed s/-/./g < $(date +%Y-%m-%d)`

C) `<<< $(date +%Y-%m-%d) | sed s/-/./g`

D) `sed s/-/./g < $(date +%Y-%m-%d)`

Explanation

The `<<<` here string sends the output of `$(date +%Y-%m-%d)` to the standard input of `sed s/-/./g`.

Question 90:

Command uptime -s shows the last date when the system was powered on, as in 2019-08-05 20:13:22. What will be the result of command uptime -s | sed -e 's/(.*) (.*)/\1/'?

A) 2019-08-05

((**Correct**))

B) 20:13:22

C) 2019

D) 08

Explanation

The sed command `sed -e 's/(.*) (.*)/\1/'` extracts the first part of the output until the space, thus resulting in `2019-08-05`.

PRACTICE TEST FIVE - LPIC-1 EXAM 101 VERSION: 5.0

90 questions | 2 hours | 90% correct required to pass

The LPIC-1 Exam 101 Version: 5.0 Practice Test is a comprehensive resource designed to prepare you for the LPIC-1 (Linux Professional Institute Certification) Exam 101. It includes practice questions that mimic the format and content of the actual test. Each **Question** comes with a detailed **Explanation** to help you understand the concepts better. This practice test is an excellent tool to harness the power of Linux and achieve LPIC-1 certification.

Question 1:

Suppose an operating system is unable to boot after adding a second SATA disk to the system. Knowing that all parts are not defective, what could be the possible cause for this error?

A) The SATA disk is defective.

B) The BIOS is not configured to boot from the newly added disk.

(Correct)

C) The SATA cable is not properly connected.

D) The power supply unit is insufficient to power both disks.

Explanation

When adding a new disk, the BIOS may need to be configured to recognize and boot from it. Failure to do so could result in the system attempting to boot from the wrong disk or not recognizing the new disk at all.

Question 2:

Suppose you want to make sure the external video card connected to the PCI bus of your newly acquired desktop computer really is the one advertised by the manufacturer, but opening the computer case will void the warranty. What command could be used to list the details of the video card, as they were detected by the operating system?

A) `lsusb`

B) `lspci`

(Correct)

C) `lsblk`

D) `lsmod`

Explanation

The `lspci` command lists all PCI devices detected by the

system, including the external video card connected to the PCI bus.

Question 3:

The following line is part of the output generated by command lspci:

`*03:00.0 RAID bus controller: LSI Logic / Symbios Logic MegaRAID SAS 2208 [Thunderbolt] (rev 05)*`

What command should you execute to identify the kernel module in use for this specific device?

A) `lsmod`

B) `modinfo`

(Correct)

C) `modprobe`

D) `dmesg`

Explanation

The `modinfo` command provides information about a kernel module, including the module in use for a specific device.

Question 4:

The boot process of a Linux machine ends up with the following message:

`*ALERT! /dev/sda3 does not exist. Dropping to a shell!*`

What is the likely cause of this problem?

A) The root filesystem is corrupt.

B) The hard drive containing /dev/sda3 is physically disconnected.

(Correct)

C) The bootloader configuration points to the wrong root filesystem.

D) The kernel cannot recognize the filesystem type of /dev/sda3.

Explanation

The message indicates that the specified device `/dev/sda3` does not exist, likely because the hard drive containing it is physically disconnected or not detected by the system.

Question 5:

The bootloader will present a list of operating systems to choose from when more than one operating system is installed on the machine. However, a newly installed operating system can overwrite the MBR of the hard disk, erasing the first stage of the bootloader and making the other operating system inaccessible. Why would this not happen on a machine equipped with a UEFI firmware?

A) UEFI firmware stores bootloader information in a separate partition.

(Correct)

B) UEFI firmware prohibits writing to the MBR by non-UEFI operating systems.

C) UEFI firmware automatically restores the MBR upon detecting changes.

D) UEFI firmware encrypts the MBR to prevent unauthorized

modifications.

Explanation

Unlike BIOS systems where the bootloader is typically installed in the Master Boot Record (MBR) of the disk, UEFI firmware uses the EFI System Partition (ESP) to store bootloader information. This partition is separate from the MBR, so installing a new operating system does not overwrite the bootloader information of existing systems.

Question 6:

What is a common consequence of installing a custom kernel without providing an appropriate initramfs image?

A) The system boots faster due to reduced initialization steps.

B) Some hardware components may not be initialized correctly at boot time.

(Correct)

C) Kernel panic occurs immediately after selecting the custom kernel.

D) The bootloader skips the kernel selection menu during startup.

Explanation

The initramfs (initial RAM filesystem) contains essential files and drivers required to mount the root filesystem. Without an appropriate initramfs image, certain hardware components necessary for booting may not be initialized correctly, leading to boot failure or system instability.

Question 7:

In a systemd based system, what command must be executed to enable activation of the units sshd.service during system initialization?

A) `systemctl enable sshd.service`

(Correct)

B) `systemctl start sshd.service`

C) `systemctl add sshd.service`

D) `systemctl activate sshd.service`

Explanation

The `systemctl enable` command in systemd-based systems is used to enable the automatic activation of units during system initialization. Therefore, `systemctl enable sshd.service` would enable the activation of the `sshd.service` unit during system startup.

Question 8:

In a SysV based system, suppose the default runlevel defined in /etc/inittab is 3, but the system always starts in runlevel 1. What is the probable cause for that?

A) Incorrect permissions on /etc/inittab

B) Misconfigured kernel parameters

C) Improperly configured bootloader

D) Faulty runlevel initialization scripts

(Correct)

Explanation

Runlevel initialization scripts, typically located in directories like `/etc/rc.d`, control the system's behavior during startup. If there's a fault in these scripts, the system may fail to transition to the desired runlevel, resulting in the observed behavior.

Question 9:

Although the file /sbin/init can be found in systemd based systems, it is only a symbolic link to another executable file. In such systems, what is the file pointed by /sbin/init?

A) /usr/lib/systemd/systemd

(Correct)

B) /bin/systemctl

C) /usr/bin/systemd

D) /lib/systemd/systemd

Explanation

In systemd-based systems, `/sbin/init` is typically a symbolic link to the systemd init system executable, which is located at `/usr/lib/systemd/systemd`.

Question 10:

How can the default system target be verified in a systemd based system?

A) `systemctl get-default`

(Correct)

B) `systemctl show-default`

C) `systemctl default`

D) `systemctl status default.target`

Explanation

The `systemctl get-default` command is used to display the default system target in systemd-based systems. It directly retrieves the configured default target.

Question 11:

When manually mounting a filesystem, under which directory should it usually be mounted?

A) /mnt

(Correct)

B) /media

C) /var

D) /opt

Explanation

When manually mounting a filesystem, it is typically mounted under the `/mnt` directory unless a different mount point is specified.

Question 12:

What is the smallest unit inside of a Volume Group?

A) Physical Extent (PE)

(Correct)

B) Logical Volume (LV)

C) Volume Group (VG)

D) Partition

Explanation

The Physical Extent (PE) is the smallest unit inside of a Volume Group in LVM (Logical Volume Manager).

Question 13:

From a GRUB 2 or GRUB Legacy menu, how can you enter the GRUB Shell?

A) Press 'S'

B) Press 'Tab'

C) Press 'Esc'

D) Press 'C'

(Correct)

Explanation

From a GRUB 2 or GRUB Legacy menu, you can enter the GRUB Shell by pressing the 'C' key.

Question 14:

What is the smallest unit inside of a Volume Group?

A) Physical Extent

(Correct)

B) Logical Volume

C) Physical Volume

D) Filesystem

Explanation

In LVM (Logical Volume Manager), the smallest unit inside of a Volume Group is called a Physical Extent (PE).

Question 15:

Imagine you have a disk identified as /dev/sda with multiple partitions. Which command can be used to find out which is the boot partition on a system?

A) blkid /dev/sda

(Correct)

B) fdisk -l /dev/sda

C) mount

D) lsblk

Explanation

The `blkid` command can be used to display information about block devices, including the UUID and filesystem type of partitions. By running `blkid /dev/sda`, you can identify the boot partition based on its filesystem type and possibly its label or UUID.

Question 16:

Which command can be used to find out the UUID of a partition?

A) uuid

B) lsblk

C) blkid

(Correct)

D) fdisk

Explanation

The `blkid` command displays information about block devices, including their UUIDs. Running `blkid` without arguments will show the UUIDs of all available block devices, or you can specify a specific device like `/dev/sda1` to see its UUID.

Question 17:

What command should you run to make the changes fully effective?

A) ldconfig

(Correct)

B) update-ld

C) ldupdate

D) configure-ld

Explanation

`ldconfig` updates the necessary links and cache to the most recent shared libraries located in the directories specified in `/etc/ld.so.conf`.

Question 18:

What command would you use to list the shared libraries required by kill?

A) ldd kill

(Correct)

B) listlibs kill

C) sharedlibs kill

D) shlibdeps kill

Explanation

The `ldd` command lists the shared libraries required by an executable or shared object.

Question 19:

objdump is a command line utility that displays information from object files. Check if it is installed in your system with which objdump. If it is not, please, install it. Use objdump with the -p (or --private-headers) option and grep to print the dependencies of glibc:

A) objdump -p /lib/libc.so.6 | grep NEEDED

(Correct)

B) objdump -p /usr/lib/libc.so.6 | grep DEPENDENCIES

C) objdump -p /lib/libc.so.6 | grep DEPENDENCIES

D) objdump -p /usr/lib/libc.so.6 | grep NEEDED

Explanation

The `objdump` command with the `-p` option displays the private headers of a binary file. `grep NEEDED` filters the output to display only the dependencies.

Question 20:

What is the command to install a package named package.deb

using dpkg?

A) dpkg -i package.deb

(Correct)

B) dpkg -install package.deb

C) dpkg -u package.deb

D) dpkg -install-package package.deb

Explanation

The `-i` option in dpkg stands for "install", and it is used to install a package from a .deb file.

Question 21:

Using dpkg-query, find which package contains a file named 7zr.1.gz.

A) dpkg-query -S 7zr.1.gz

B) dpkg-query -L 7zr.1.gz

C) dpkg-query --search 7zr.1.gz

(Correct)

D) dpkg-query --find 7zr.1.gz

Explanation

The `--search` or `-S` option in dpkg-query is used to search for packages containing a specific file.

Question 22:

Can you remove a package called unzip from the system using dpkg -r unzip if the package file-roller depends on it? If not, what would be the correct way to do it?

A) Yes, you can forcefully remove it.

B) No, you cannot remove it with dpkg -r.

(Correct)

C) Yes, you can remove it without any issues.

D) Yes, but you need to first uninstall file-roller.

Explanation

dpkg -r removes the specified package but does not handle dependencies. Since file-roller depends on unzip, removing it with dpkg -r would cause dependency issues. Instead, you should use `apt` or `apt-get` to handle dependencies properly.

Question 23:

Using zypper, how would you disable a repository called repo-extras?

A) zypper repo-disable repo-extras

(Correct)

B) zypper disable-repo repo-extras

C) zypper repo-enable repo-extras

D) zypper enable-repo repo-extras

Explanation

The `zypper repo-disable` command is used to disable a repository.

Question 24:

If you have a .repo file describing a new repository, where this file should be put so that it is recognized by DNF?

A) /etc/yum.repos.d/

(Correct)

B) /etc/dnf.repos.d/

C) /etc/repos.d/

D) /etc/package.repos.d/

Explanation

DNF, the successor to Yum, looks for repository configuration files in the /etc/yum.repos.d/ directory.

Question 25:

How would you use zypper to find out which package owns the file /usr/sbin/swapon?

A) zypper search /usr/sbin/swapon

B) zypper what-provides /usr/sbin/swapon

C) zypper list --file /usr/sbin/swapon

D) zypper provides /usr/sbin/swapon

(Correct)

Explanation

The `zypper provides` command is used to find out which package provides a specific file.

Question 26:

Which disk image type consumes space only as new data is written to the disk?

A) RAW

B) Sparse

(Correct)

C) Pre-allocated

D) Compressed

Explanation

B) Sparse (or thin-provisioned) disk images consume space only as new data is written to the disk, allowing for dynamic allocation of disk space.

Question 27:

What CPU extensions are necessary on an x86 based hardware platform that will run fully virtualized guests?

A) VT-x

(Correct)

B) AMD-V

C) SSE

D) NX

Explanation

VT-x (Intel Virtualization Technology) is necessary for Intel-based hardware platforms to run fully virtualized guests.

AMD-based platforms require AMD-V.

Question 28:

Use the man system to determine how to tell apropos to output a brief command so that it outputs only a brief usage message and then exits.

A) apropos -b

B) apropos --brief

(Correct)

C) apropos -s

D) apropos --short

Explanation

According to the man page of apropos, the `--brief` option is used to output a brief command, displaying only a brief usage message and then exiting.

Question 29:

Use the man system to determine which copyright license is assigned to the grep command.

A) GPL

(Correct)

B) BSD

C) MIT

D) Apache License

Explanation

The GNU grep command is licensed under the GNU General Public License (GPL), which can be confirmed by consulting its man page or the documentation.

Question 30:

Identify the hardware architecture and Linux kernel version being used on your computer in an easy-to-read output format.

A) uname -a

(Correct)

B) hardwareinfo

C) sysinfo

D) lspci

Explanation

The `uname -a` command displays system information, including the hardware architecture and Linux kernel version, in an easy-to-read format.

Question 31:

What is the purpose of the `uniq` command in Linux?

A) To count the number of lines in a file.

B) To display the contents of a file.

C) To list and count matching strings in a file.

(Correct)

D) To edit files using pre-defined patterns.

Explanation

The correct answer is C) The `uniq` command is used to list and count matching strings in a file.

Question 32:

Which command is used to replace characters and remove repeating characters in Linux?

A) `cut`

B) `paste`

C) `tr`

(Correct)

D) `split`

Explanation

The correct answer is C) The `tr` command is used to replace characters and remove repeating characters.

Question 33:

Based on the previous listing:

$ ls

file1.txt file2.txt file3.txt file4.txt

What files would be displayed by the following command?

$ ls file.txt*

Which wildcard would help to delete all the contents of this directory?

A) file*.txt

(Correct)

B) file?.txt

C) file

D) file[]

Explanation

The * wildcard matches any string of characters, so it will match all filenames that start with 'file' and end with '.txt'.

Question 34:

Complete the command by adding the appropriate digits and characters in the square brackets that would list all the content above:

$ ls file[].txt

What characters should be added in the square brackets?

A) *

(Correct)

B) ?

C) []

D) {}

Explanation

The * wildcard matches any string of characters, so it will match all filenames ending with '.txt'.

Question 35:

Consider the following listing:

$ find /home/frank/Documents/ -type d

/home/frank/Documents/

/home/frank/Documents/animal

/home/frank/Documents/animal/domestic

/home/frank/Documents/animal/wild

What kind of files would this command output?

A) Text files

B) Directories

(Correct)

C) Executable files

D) Hidden files

Explanation

The `-type d` option in the `find` command specifies that it should only output directories.

Question 36:

Based on the previous listing:

$ find /home/frank/Documents/ -type d

/home/frank/Documents/

/home/frank/Documents/animal

/home/frank/Documents/animal/domestic

/home/frank/Documents/animal/wild

In which directory does the search begin?

A) /home

B) /home/frank

C) /home/frank/Documents

(Correct)

D) /home/frank/Documents/animal

Explanation

The search begins in the directory /home/frank/Documents.

Question 37:

The Linux kernel keeps symbolic links in `/proc/PID/fd/` to every file opened by a process, where PID is the identification number of the corresponding process. How could the system administrator use that directory to verify the location of log files opened by nginx, supposing its PID is 1234?

A) `ls -l /proc/1234/fd | grep log`

B) `ls -l /proc/1234/fd | grep nginx`

C) `ls -l /proc/1234/fd | grep /var/log/nginx`

(Correct)

D) `ls -l /proc/1234/fd | grep /var/log`

Explanation

This command lists the file descriptors of process 1234 and searches for those associated with files in the `/var/log/nginx` directory, which are likely the log files opened by nginx.

Question 38:

It's possible to do arithmetic calculations using only shell builtin commands, but floating-point calculations require specific programs, like `bc` (basic calculator). With `bc`, it's even possible to specify the number of decimal places, with parameter scale. However, `bc` accepts operations only through its standard input, usually entered in interactive mode. Using a Here string, how can the floating-point operation `scale=6; 1/3` be sent to the standard input of `bc`?

A) `bc <<< "scale=6; 1/3"`

(Correct)

B) `echo "scale=6; 1/3" | bc`

C) `scale=6; 1/3 | bc`

D) `bc -l <<< "scale=6; 1/3"`

Explanation

This command uses a Here string (`<<<`) to send the specified expression to `bc`'s standard input.

Question 39:

It's convenient to save the execution date of actions performed by automated scripts. Command `date +%Y-%m-%d` shows the current date in year-month-day format. How can the output of such a command be stored in a shell variable called `TODAY` using command substitution?

A) `TODAY=$(date +%Y-%m-%d)`

(Correct)

B) `$(TODAY=date +%Y-%m-%d)`

C) `date +%Y-%m-%d > TODAY`

D) `TODAY=date +%Y-%m-%d`

Explanation

Command substitution with `$(...)` allows the output of a command (`date +%Y-%m-%d`) to be assigned to the variable `TODAY`.

Question 40:

Using command `echo`, how can the contents of variable `TODAY` be sent to the standard input of command `sed s/-/./g`?

A) `echo $TODAY | sed s/-/./g`

(Correct)

B) `echo $TODAY > sed s/-/./g`

C) `echo $TODAY | > sed s/-/./g`

D) `echo $TODAY > | sed s/-/./g`

Explanation

The `|` pipe symbol sends the output of `echo $TODAY` to the standard input of `sed s/-/./g`.

Question 41:

Which key combination is used as the command prefix in GNU Screen?

A) Ctrl + a

(Correct)

B) Ctrl + b

C) Ctrl + c

D) Ctrl + s

Explanation

In GNU Screen, commands are typically initiated by pressing Ctrl + a followed by another character to execute the desired action.

Question 42:

How can you detach a session from its terminal in GNU Screen?

A) Ctrl + a - d

(Correct)

B) Ctrl + b - d

C) Ctrl + a - x

D) Ctrl + b - x

Explanation

Pressing Ctrl + a - d detaches the screen session from the current terminal, allowing it to continue running in the background.

Question 43:

Which command is used to create a new session in tmux with a specified session and window name?

A) tmux new-session -s "session_name" -n "window_name"

B) tmux create-session -s "session_name" -w "window_name"

C) tmux new -s "session_name" -n "window_name"

(Correct)

D) tmux start -s "session_name" -w "window_name"

Explanation

The tmux command followed by `new` option allows you to create a new session, `-s` option specifies the session name, and `-n` option specifies the window name.

Question 44:

How can you rename a window in tmux?

A) Ctrl + b - r

B) Ctrl + b - ,

(Correct)

C) Ctrl + b - n

D) Ctrl + b - $

Explanation

Pressing Ctrl + b followed by `,` allows you to rename the current window in tmux.

Question 45:

What is the key combination to split a window vertically in tmux?

A) Ctrl + b - |

(Correct)

B) Ctrl + b - "

C) Ctrl + b - %

D) Ctrl + b - x

Explanation

Pressing Ctrl + b followed by `|` splits the tmux window vertically into two panes.

Question 46:

How can you list all sessions in tmux?

A) Ctrl + b - s

B) tmux ls

C) Ctrl + b - l

D) All of the above

(Correct)

Explanation

All of the mentioned options can be used to list all sessions in tmux.

Question 47:

What is the purpose of the copy mode in tmux?

A) To create a backup of all active sessions

B) To scroll through the terminal output of a window

C) To copy and paste text between tmux windows

(Correct)

D) To share a session with other users

Explanation

Copy mode in tmux allows users to select and copy text from the terminal output for pasting into other tmux windows or external applications.

Question 48:

Which configuration file is used to customize tmux settings at the user level?

A) /etc/tmux.conf

B) ~/.tmux.conf

(Correct)

C) /usr/share/doc/tmux/example_tmux.conf

D) /usr/local/etc/tmux.conf

Explanation

The `~/.tmux.conf` file is used to customize tmux settings at the user level. It overrides the system-wide configuration file located at `/etc/tmux.conf`.

Question 49:

What command is used to attach to a detached tmux session?

A) tmux reconnect

B) tmux attach

(Correct)

C) tmux connect

D) tmux reattach

Explanation

The `tmux attach` command is used to attach to a detached tmux session and resume working within it.

Question 50:

How can you resize a tmux pane by one line?

A) Ctrl + b - Alt + arrow key

B) Ctrl + b - Ctrl + arrow key

(Correct)

C) Ctrl + b - ? , ? , ? , ?

D) Ctrl + b - {

Explanation

Pressing Ctrl + b followed by Ctrl + arrow key allows you to resize a tmux pane by one line.

Question 51:

What is the purpose of a terminal multiplexer's copy mode?

A) To create multiple independent terminal sessions

B) To scroll through the terminal output

C) To manage windows and panes within a session

D) To copy and paste text between terminal sessions

(Correct)

Explanation

Copy mode in a terminal multiplexer allows users to select and copy text from the terminal output of one session or pane to paste into another session or external application.

Question 52:

In a preemptive multi-tasking system, what happens when a lower priority process is occupying the processor and a higher priority process is queued to be executed?

A) The lower priority process continues to execute until it voluntarily yields the CPU

B) The lower priority process is paused, and the higher priority process is executed

(Correct)

C) The higher priority process is queued until the lower priority process completes its execution

D) Both processes continue to execute simultaneously

Explanation

In a preemptive multi-tasking system, the operating system has the capability to pause a lower priority process and allow a higher priority process to execute, ensuring that critical tasks are performed promptly.

Question 53:

What PIDs have real-time priorities?

A) 12 and 17

B) 12 and 14

C) 12, 14, and 17

D) 14 and 17

(Correct)

Explanation

PIDs 12 and 17 have real-time priorities as indicated by the "rt" value in the PR column.

Question 54:

Which PID has higher priority?

A) 2

B) 9

C) 10

(Correct)

D) 12

Explanation

Among the listed PIDs, PID 10 has the highest priority as indicated by its higher "PRI" value (80).

Question 55:

After trying to renice a process with renice, the following error happens:

"renice: failed to set priority for 21704 (process ID): Permission denied".

What is the probable cause for the error?

A) The process ID does not exist

B) The renice command syntax is incorrect

C) The user does not have sufficient permissions to change the process priority

(Correct)

D) The process priority is already set to the maximum level

Explanation

The error message "Permission denied" indicates that the user attempting to change the process priority does not have the necessary permissions to do so.

Question 56:

What is the purpose of a Btrfs subvolume?

A) To allocate fixed space on a drive

B) To encrypt data on disk

C) To store backups separately

D) To mount as a separate filesystem

(Correct)

Explanation

A Btrfs subvolume is like a directory that can be mounted as (and treated like) a separate filesystem.

Question 57:

Suppose /dev/sdb1 is an ext2 filesystem. How can you convert it to ext3, and at the same time reset its mount count and change its label to UserData?

A) `tune2fs -j -L UserData /dev/sdb1`

B) `tune2fs -j -c 0 -L UserData /dev/sdb1`

(Correct)

C) `tune2fs -m 0 -j -L UserData /dev/sdb1`

D) `tune2fs -m 0 -j -l UserData /dev/sdb1`

Explanation

The `-j` option converts the filesystem to ext3, `-c 0` resets the mount count, and `-L UserData` changes the label to UserData.

Question 58:

How can you check for errors on an XFS filesystem, without repairing any damage found?

A) `xfs_check -n /dev/sda1`

B) `xfs_repair -n /dev/sda1`

(Correct)

C) `xfs_admin -n /dev/sda1`

D) `xfs_db -n /dev/sda1`

Explanation

The `-n` option in `xfs_repair` performs a dry run, checking for errors without actually making any repairs.

Question 59:

Consider you have an ext4 filesystem on /dev/sda1 with the following parameters, obtained with tune2fs: Mount count: 8, Maximum mount count: -1. What will happen at the next boot if the command `tune2fs -c 9 /dev/sda1` is issued?

A) The filesystem will be checked for errors at every boot.

(Correct)

B) The mount count will be reset to 0.

C) The filesystem will be automatically mounted without any checks.

D) The maximum mount count will be set to 9.

Explanation

By setting the mount count to 9, the filesystem will be checked for errors at every boot, as it exceeds the previous mount count.

Question 60:

How can you find out the UUID of a filesystem under /dev/sdb1?

A) `lsblk -f /dev/sdb1`

B) `blkid /dev/sdb1`

(Correct)

C) `uuid /dev/sdb1`

D) `udevadm info -q all /dev/sdb1`

Explanation

The `blkid` command lists information about block devices, including their UUIDs.

Question 61:

How can you use mount to remount as read-only an

exFAT filesystem with the UUID 6e2c12e3-472d-4bac-a257-c49ac07f3761, mounted at /mnt/data?

A) `mount -o ro,remount UUID=6e2c12e3-472d-4bac-a257-c49ac07f3761 /mnt/data`

B) `mount -o remount,ro UUID=6e2c12e3-472d-4bac-a257-c49ac07f3761 /mnt/data`

(Correct)

C) `mount -o remount,ro /mnt/data`

D) `mount -o ro,remount /mnt/data`

Explanation

The `mount -o remount,ro` command is used to remount a filesystem as read-only. By specifying the UUID and mount point, it specifically remounts the exFAT filesystem at /mnt/data.

Question 62:

How can you get a list of all ext3 and ntfs filesystems currently mounted on a system?

A) `mount -t ext3,ntfs`

B) `mount | grep -E 'ext3|ntfs'`

(Correct)

C) `mount -t ext3 && mount -t ntfs`

D) `mount -l ext3 -l ntfs`

Explanation

The `mount` command lists all mounted filesystems, and

`grep` filters the output to include only lines containing "ext3" or "ntfs".

Question 63:

Consider the following entry in /etc/fstab: `/dev/sdc1 /backup ext4 noatime,nouser,async`. Can a user mount this filesystem with the command `mount /backup`? Why?

A) Yes, because `noauto` is not specified.

B) No, because `nouser` prevents regular users from mounting it.

(Correct)

C) Yes, because `async` overrides `nouser`.

D) No, because `ext4` filesystems cannot be mounted by users.

Explanation

The `nouser` option in `/etc/fstab` prevents regular users from mounting the filesystem. Therefore, users cannot mount it with the `mount /backup` command.

Question 64:

What does the command `chgrp users file.txt` do?

A) Changes the ownership of the file to the group `users`.

B) Changes the group ownership of the file to the group `users`.

(Correct)

C) Changes the ownership of the file to the user `users`.

D) Changes the group ownership of the file to the user `users`.

Explanation

The `chgrp` command is used to change the group ownership of a file or directory.

Question 65:

Which command is used to create a new directory?

A) newdir

B) create

C) mkdir

(Correct)

D) touchdir

Explanation

The `mkdir` command is used to create a new directory.

Question 66:

Let us assume a file named test.sh is a shell script with the following permissions and ownership: `-rwxr-sr-x 1 carol root 33 Dec 11 10:36 test.sh` - What are the permissions for the owner of the file?

A) rwx

(Correct)

B) rws

C) r-x

D) r-xr

Explanation

The permissions `rwx` indicate that the owner (`carol`) has read, write, and execute permissions.

Question 67:

Using the octal notation, what would the syntax of chmod be to "unset" the special permission granted to this file?

A) chmod 755 test.sh

B) chmod 775 test.sh

(Correct)

C) chmod 7555 test.sh

D) chmod 744 test.sh

Explanation

The setuid bit is represented by the octal value of 4. Therefore, to unset it, we need to change the permissions from `775` to `755`.

Question 68:

Consider this file: `brw-rw---- 1 root disk 8, 17 Dec 21 18:51 /dev/sdb1`. Which type of file is sdb1? Who can write to it?

A) Block device; only root and users in the disk group can write to it.

(Correct)

B) Character device; only root and users in the disk group can write to it.

C) Block device; only root can write to it.

D) Character device; only root can write to it.

Explanation

The `b` at the beginning indicates it's a block device file. The permissions `rw` for the group indicate that users in the `disk` group can write to it, in addition to the owner (`root`).

Question 69:

Consider the following 4 files:

Another_Directory: `drwxr-xr-t`

foo.bar: `----r--r--`

HugeFile.zip: `-rw-rw-r--`

Sample_Directory: `drwxr-sr-x`

Choose the corresponding permissions for each file and directory using octal mode using the 4-digit notation.

A) Another_Directory: 1755, foo.bar: 0444, HugeFile.zip: 0664, Sample_Directory: 2755

(Correct)

B) Another_Directory: 1555, foo.bar: 0222, HugeFile.zip: 0662, Sample_Directory: 2735

C) Another_Directory: 1766, foo.bar: 0111, HugeFile.zip: 0664, Sample_Directory: 2775

D) Another_Directory: 1711, foo.bar: 0777, HugeFile.zip: 0666, Sample_Directory: 2772

Explanation

Another_Directory: `drwxr-xr-t` converts to 1755 in octal

mode. The `t` at the end indicates the sticky bit is set.

foo.bar: `----r--r--` converts to 0444 in octal mode.

HugeFile.zip: `-rw-rw-r--` converts to 0664 in octal mode.

Sample_Directory: `drwxr-sr-x` converts to 2755 in octal mode. The `s` at the group permission indicates the setgid bit is set.

Question 70:

Command less is the default paginator for displaying long text files in the shell environment. By typing /, a regular expression can be entered in the search prompt to jump to the first corresponding match. In order to stay in the current document position and only highlight the corresponding matches, what key combination should be entered at the search prompt?

A) H

B) F

C) N

(Correct)

D) G

Explanation

Typing `N` at the search prompt in less will highlight all occurrences of the searched term without moving the cursor.

Question 71:

In less, how would it be possible to filter the output so only lines which match a regular expression get displayed?

A) `/pattern`

B) `&pattern`

(Correct)

C) `|pattern`

D) `!pattern`

Explanation

Typing `&pattern` at the prompt in less filters the output to display only lines that match the specified regular expression pattern.

Question 72:

Command last shows a listing of last logged in users, including their origin IPs. How would the egrep command be used to filter last output, showing only occurrences of an IPv4 address, discarding any additional information in the corresponding line?

A) `last | egrep -o '\b(?:[0-9]{1,3}\.){3}[0-9]{1,3}\b'`

(Correct)

B) `last | egrep -o '[0-9]+\.[0-9]+\.[0-9]+\.[0-9]+'`

C) `last | egrep -o '\b(?:[0-9]{1,3}\.){2}[0-9]{1,3}\.[0-9]{1,3}\b'`

D) `last | egrep -o '[0-9]{1,3}\.[0-9]{1,3}\.[0-9]{1,3}\.[0-9]{1,3}'`

Explanation

This egrep command with the `-o` option uses a regular expression to extract only IPv4 addresses from the output of the last command, discarding any additional information on the line.

Question 73:

What option should be given to grep in order to correctly filter the output generated by command find executed with option -print0?

A) `-z`

(Correct)

B) `-0`

C) `-null`

D) `-print0`

Explanation

When using the `-print0` option with find, it separates filenames with null characters instead of newlines. To correctly filter such output with grep, the `-z` option should be used to interpret null characters as line terminators.

Question 74:

vi is most used as an editor for configuration files and source code, where indentation helps to identify sections of text. A selection can be indented to the left by pressing < and to the right by pressing >. What keys should be pressed in normal mode to indent the current selection three steps to the left?

A) `<<<<`

B) `<<<<`

C) `3<<`

(Correct)

D) `3<`

Explanation

Pressing `3<<` in normal mode will indent the current selection three steps to the left.

Question 75:

An entire line can be selected by pressing V in vi normal mode. However, the terminating newline character is also included. What keys should be pressed in normal mode to select from the starting character until, but not including, the newline character?

A) `vy`

B) `V$`

C) `V^`

D) `Vg_`

(Correct)

Explanation

Pressing `Vg_` in normal mode will select from the starting character until, but not including, the newline character.

Question 76:

How should vi be executed in the command line to open ~/.bash_profile and jump straight to the last line?

A) `vi ~/.bash_profile +$`

(Correct)

B) `vi +$ ~/.bash_profile`

C) `vi + ~/.bash_profile`

D) `vi ~/.bash_profile +$`

Explanation

Executing `vi ~/.bash_profile +$` in the command line will open the file ~/.bash_profile and jump straight to the last line.

Question 77:

During the course of this lesson, you were trying out some commands in parted but, by mistake, deleted the 3rd partition on your hard disk. You know that it came after a 250 MB UEFI partition and a 4 GB swap partition, and was 10 GB in size. Which command can you use to recover it?

A) `mkpart primary 4000M 14000M`

B) `mkpart primary 250M 14000M`

C) `mkpart primary 0 14000M`

D) `mkpart primary 250M 10250M`

(Correct)

Explanation

To recreate the partition, you need to specify the correct start and end points. Assuming the previous partition was 10 GB in size and came after a 250 MB partition, you would start the new partition at 250 MB and end it at 10.25 GB.

Question 78:

Imagine you have a 4 GB unused partition on /dev/sda3. Using fdisk, what would be the sequence of operations to turn it into an active swap partition?

A) Create a new partition, format it as swap, and activate it.

B) Activate the partition and format it as swap.

C) Format the partition as swap and activate it.

D) Create a new partition, activate it, and set its type to swap.

(Correct)

Explanation

The sequence of operations would be to first create a new partition using `fdisk`, then activate it using `swapon`, and finally set its type to swap using `mkswap`.

Question 79:

What is the purpose of Btrfs filesystem's copy-on-write feature?

A) To overwrite data directly on disk

B) To reduce the chances of data loss in case of a crash

(Correct)

C) To compress files on-the-fly

D) To encrypt data on disk

Explanation

The copy-on-write feature of Btrfs filesystem ensures that new data is written to free space on disk before the old data is discarded, reducing the chances of data loss in case of a crash.

Question 80:

Which utility is used to create a Btrfs filesystem?

A) mkfs.ext4

B) mkfs.btrfs

(Correct)

C) mkfs.xfs

D) mkfs.ntfs

Explanation

The mkfs.btrfs utility is used to create a Btrfs filesystem.

Question 81:

The initialization log is hundreds of lines long, so the output of dmesg command is often piped to a pager command — like command less — to facilitate the reading. What dmesg option will automatically paginate its output, eliminating the need to use a pager command explicitly?

A) `-n`

B) `-p`

C) `-H`

(Correct)

D) `-w`

Explanation

The `-H` option in the `dmesg` command stands for "Human-readable." When used, it formats the output in a human-readable form and automatically paginates it, eliminating the need to pipe it into a pager command like `less`.

Question 82:

On a disk formatted with the MBR partitioning scheme, which is the ID of the EFI System Partition?

A) 0xEF

(Correct)

B) 0x83

C) 0x0C

D) 0x07

Explanation

On a disk formatted with the MBR partitioning scheme, the ID of the EFI System Partition (ESP) is `0xEF`.

Question 83:

How can you set GRUB 2 to wait for 10 seconds before booting the default menu entry?

A) Set GRUB_TIMEOUT=10 in /etc/default/grub and run update-grub

(Correct)

B) Set GRUB_TIMEOUT=10 in /boot/grub/grub.cfg

C) Set GRUB_TIMEOUT=10 in /etc/grub2/grub.cfg

D) Set GRUB_TIMEOUT=10 in /boot/grub/menu.lst

Explanation

To set GRUB 2 to wait for 10 seconds before booting the default menu entry, you should edit the `/etc/default/grub` file and set `GRUB_TIMEOUT=10`, then run `update-grub` to apply the changes.

Question 84:

Use objdump with the -p (or --private-headers) option and grep to print the soname of glibc:

A) objdump -p /lib/libc.so.6 | grep SONAME

(Correct)

B) objdump -p /usr/lib/libc.so.6 | grep NAME

C) objdump -p /lib/libc.so.6 | grep SO_NAME

D) objdump -p /usr/lib/libc.so.6 | grep SO_NAME

Explanation

The `objdump` command with the `-p` option displays the private headers of a binary file. `grep SONAME` filters the output to display only the soname.

Question 85:

Using apt-file, how can you find out which package contains the file unrar?

A) apt-file search unrar

(Correct)

B) apt-file find unrar

C) apt-file locate unrar

D) apt-file query unrar

Explanation

The `apt-file search` command is used to search for packages containing a specific file.

Question 86:

Using dnf, what is the command to add a repository located at https://www.example.url/home:reponame.repo to the system?

A) dnf add-repo https://www.example.url/home:reponame.repo

B) dnf repository add https://www.example.url/home:reponame.repo

C) dnf config-manager --add-repo https://www.example.url/home:reponame.repo

(Correct)

D) dnf repo-add https://www.example.url/home:reponame.repo

Explanation

The `dnf config-manager --add-repo` command is used to add a repository to the system.

Question 87:

As a system administrator, it is required to perform regular checks to remove voluminous files. These voluminous files are located in /var and end with a .backup extension.

Write down the command, using find, to locate these files:

A) `find /var -type f -name "*.backup"`

(Correct)

B) `find /var -type d -name "*.backup"`

C) `find /var -type f -name "*.backup" -size +100M -size -1000M`

D) `find /var -type f -name "*.backup" -exec rm {} \;`

Explanation

This command uses `find` to locate files (`-type f`) with names ending in .backup (`-name "*.backup"`).

Question 88:

Command `convert image.jpeg -resize 25% small/image.jpeg` creates a smaller version of `image.jpeg` and places the resulting image in a likewise named file inside subdirectory `small`. Using `xargs`, how is it possible to perform the same command for every image listed in file `filelist.txt`?

A) `xargs -I{} convert {} -resize 25% small/{} < filelist.txt`

(Correct)

B) `xargs -I{} -resize 25% small/{} convert < filelist.txt`

C) `convert -resize 25% small/{} < filelist.txt | xargs -I{}`

D) `xargs -I{} -resize 25% small/{} convert {} < filelist.txt`

Explanation

The `-I{}` option specifies the placeholder for each filename in `filelist.txt`, allowing `xargs` to execute the `convert` command for each filename.

Question 89:

What option should be given to grep so it counts matching lines instead of displaying them?

A) `-c`

(Correct)

B) `-n`

C) `-m`

D) `-q`

Explanation

The `-c` option in grep is used to count the number of lines that match the pattern instead of displaying them.

Question 90:

Consider the following output of du -h: `216K ./somedir/anotherdir`, `224K ./somedir`, `232K .`. How much space is occupied by just the files on the current directory? How could we rewrite the command to show this information more clearly?

A) 232 KB; `du -sh`

B) 456 KB; `du -sh .`

C) 232 KB; `du -sh *`

(Correct)

D) 672 KB; `du -sh *`

Explanation

The total size of files on the current directory is 232 KB. The `du -sh *` command displays the size of each directory in the current directory.

PRACTICE TEST SIX - LPIC-1 EXAM 101 VERSION: 5.0

60 questions | 1 hour 30 minutes | 90% correct required to pass

The LPIC-1 Exam 101 Version: 5.0 Practice Test is a comprehensive resource designed to prepare you for the LPIC-1 (Linux Professional Institute Certification) Exam 101. It includes practice questions that mimic the format and content of the actual test. Each **Question** comes with a detailed **Explanation** to help you understand the concepts better. This practice test is an excellent tool to harness the power of Linux and achieve LPIC-1 certification.

Question 1:

A hard drive containing the entire filesystem of an offline machine was removed and attached to a working machine as a secondary drive. Assuming its mount point is /mnt/hd, how would journalctl be used to inspect the contents of the journal files located at /mnt/hd/var/log/journal/?

A) `journalctl -D /mnt/hd/var/log/journal/`

B) `journalctl --directory=/mnt/hd/var/log/journal/`

((**Correct**))

C) `journalctl -M /mnt/hd/var/log/journal/`

D) `journalctl --mount=/mnt/hd/var/log/journal/`

Explanation

The `journalctl` command is used to query the systemd journal logs. When inspecting logs from a different system or disk, you need to specify the directory where the journal files are located using the `--directory` or `-D` option. Therefore, option B is the correct way to inspect the journal files located at /mnt/hd/var/log/journal/.

Question 2:

How can a system reboot scheduled with the shutdown command be canceled?

A) `shutdown -c`

((**Correct**))

B) `shutdown --cancel`

C) `shutdown --abort`

D) `shutdown -a`

Explanation

The `shutdown -c` command cancels a scheduled shutdown or reboot initiated with the `shutdown` command. It stops the countdown timer and prevents the system from shutting down or rebooting.

Question 3:

From a GRUB Legacy shell, what are the commands to install GRUB to the first partition of the second disk?

A) root (hd1,0) & setup (hd1)

((**Correct**))

B) root (hd0,1) & setup (hd1)

C) root (hd1,0) & setup (hd0)

D) root (hd0,1) & setup (hd0)

Explanation

In a GRUB Legacy shell, to install GRUB to the first partition of the second disk, you would set the root device using `root (hd1,0)` and then install GRUB to the specified device with `setup (hd1)`.

Question 4:

Use objdump with the -p (or --private-headers) option and grep to print the dependencies of Bash:

A) objdump -p /bin/bash | grep NEEDED

((**Correct**))

B) objdump -p /usr/bin/bash | grep DEPENDENCIES

C) objdump -p /bin/bash | grep DEPENDENCIES

D) objdump -p /usr/bin/bash | grep NEEDED

Explanation

The `objdump` command with the `-p` option displays the private headers of a binary file. `grep NEEDED` filters the output to display only the dependencies.

Question 5:

Using apt-cache, what is the command to show information for the package gimp?

A) apt-cache show gimp

((**Correct**))

B) apt-cache info gimp

C) apt-cache package gimp

D) apt-cache view gimp

Explanation

The `apt-cache show` command displays detailed information about a specific package.

Question 6:

How can you use zypper to check if the package unzip is installed?

A) zypper search unzip

B) zypper list unzip

C) zypper info unzip

((**Correct**))

D) zypper status unzip

Explanation

The `zypper info` command displays detailed information about a package, including its installation status.

Question 7:

Using yum, find out which package provides the file /bin/wget.

A) yum provides /bin/wget

((**Correct**))

B) yum search /bin/wget

C) yum whatprovides /bin/wget

D) yum search wget

Explanation

The `yum provides` command is used to find out which package provides a specific file.

Question 8:

A mission-critical server installation that will require the fastest performance will likely use what type of virtualization?

A) Full virtualization

B) Paravirtualization

C) Hardware-assisted virtualization

((**Correct**))

D) Containerization

Explanation

Hardware-assisted virtualization, such as Intel VT-x or AMD-V, provides the fastest performance for virtualized environments, making it suitable for mission-critical server installations.

Question 9:

Two virtual machines that have been cloned from the same template and that utilize D-Bus are performing erratically. They both have separate hostnames and network configuration settings. What command would be used to determine if each of the virtual machines have different D-Bus Machine IDs?

A) dbus-daemon --print-machine-id

((**Correct**))

B) dbus-monitor --machine-id

C) dbus-uuidgen --ensure

D) systemctl show dbus.service

Explanation

The `dbus-daemon --print-machine-id` command prints the D-Bus Machine ID, allowing you to determine if each virtual machine has a different ID.

Question 10:

Use the export command to add a new directory to your path (this will not survive a reboot).

A) `export PATH=$PATH:/new/directory`

((**Correct**))

B) `export PATH:/new/directory`

C) `PATH=/new/directory:$PATH`

D) `PATH:/new/directory:$PATH`

Explanation

To add a new directory to the PATH environment variable, you need to use the `export` command followed by the variable name (`PATH`) and its updated value (`$PATH:/new/directory`).

Question 11:

Use the unset command to delete the PATH variable. Try running a command (like sudo cat /etc/shadow) using sudo. What happened? Why? (Exiting your shell will return you to your original state.)

A) The command runs successfully.

B) Permission denied error occurs.

C) Command not found error occurs.

((**Correct**))

D) Command runs but with limited functionality.

Explanation

When you unset the PATH variable, the system won't be able to locate the sudo command in the directories specified in the PATH. As a result, you'll get a "Command not found" error when trying to run `sudo`.

Question 12:

How can you view the number of lines in a file and recreate the file with each line prepended by its line number?

A) Using the `wc` command.

B) Using the `nl` command.

((**Correct**))

C) Using the `sort` command.

D) Using the `head` command.

Explanation

The correct answer is B) The `nl` command is used to number lines in a file and recreate the file with each line prepended by its line number.

Question 13:

Explore your local /etc/passwd file with the grep, sed, head and tail commands per the tasks below: Which users have access to a Bash shell?

A) `grep -e '/bash' /etc/passwd`

B) `grep '/bash' /etc/passwd`

C) `grep '/bash' /etc/passwd | cut -d: -f1`

D) `grep -e '/bash' /etc/passwd | cut -d: -f1`

((**Correct**))

Explanation

This command searches for lines containing '/bash' in the / etc/passwd file, which typically indicates users with access to a Bash shell. Then, it uses `cut -d: -f1` to extract only the usernames from those lines.

Question 14:

An analysis of the sizes of these files reveals that they range from 100M to 1000M. Complete the previous command with this new information, so that you may locate those backup files ranging from 100M to 1000M:

A) `find /var -type f -name "*.backup" -size +100M -size -1000M`

((**Correct**))

B) `find /var -type f -name "*.backup" -size +100M`

C) `find /var -type f -name "*.backup" -size 100M-1000M`

D) `find /var -type f -name "*.backup" -exec rm {} \;`

Explanation

This command uses the `-size` option to specify the size range of the files.

Question 15:

Complete this command, with the delete action so that these files will be removed:

A) `find /var -type f -name "*.backup" -delete`

B) `find /var -type f -name "*.backup" -exec rm {} \;`

((**Correct**))

C) `find /var -type f -name "*.backup" -delete -exec rm {} \;`

D) `find /var -type f -name "*.backup" -exec rm -f {} \;`

Explanation

This command uses `-exec rm {} \;` to execute the `rm` command for each found file.

Question 16:

In the /var directory, there exist four backup files:

db-jan-2018.backup

db-feb-2018.backup

db-march-2018.backup

db-apr-2018.backup

Using tar, specify the command that would create an archive file with the name db-firstquarter-2018.backup.tar:

A) `tar cvf db-firstquarter-2018.backup.tar db-jan-2018.backup db-feb-2018.backup db-march-2018.backup`

((**Correct**))

B) `tar cvf db-firstquarter-2018.backup.tar.gz db-jan-2018.backup db-feb-2018.backup db-march-2018.backup`

C) `tar cvf db-firstquarter-2018.backup.tar db-jan-2018.backup db-feb-2018.backup db-march-2018.backup db-apr-2018.backup`

D) `tar cvf db-firstquarter-2018.backup.tar.gz db-jan-2018.backup db-feb-2018.backup db-march-2018.backup db-apr-2018.backup`

Explanation

This command creates a tar archive named db-firstquarter-2018.backup.tar containing the specified backup files.

Question 17:

A simple backup routine periodically creates an image of partition `/dev/sda1` with `dd </dev/sda1 > sda1.img`. To perform future data integrity checks, the routine also generates a SHA1 hash of the file with `sha1sum < sda1.img > sda1.sha1`. By adding pipes and command `tee`, how would these two commands be combined into one?

A) `dd </dev/sda1 | tee sda1.img | sha1sum > sda1.sha1`

((**Correct**))

B) `dd </dev/sda1 > sda1.img | tee | sha1sum > sda1.sha1`

C) `dd </dev/sda1 > sda1.img | tee sda1.sha1 | sha1sum`

D) `tee sda1.img | dd </dev/sda1 | sha1sum > sda1.sha1`

Explanation

`tee` copies the output to both `sda1.img` and `sha1sum`, allowing the commands to be combined into one.

Question 18:

Command `tar` is used to archive many files into a single file, preserving directory structure. Option `-T` allows to specify a file containing the paths to be archived. For example, `find /etc -type f | tar -cJ -f /srv/backup/etc.tar.xz -T -` creates a compressed tar file `etc.tar.xz` from the list provided by command `find` (option `-T -` indicates the standard input as the path list). In order to avoid possible parsing errors due to paths containing spaces, what command options should be present for `find` and `tar`?

A) `find /etc -type f -print0 | tar -cJ -f /srv/backup/etc.tar.xz --null -T -`

((**Correct**))

B) `find /etc -type f -print0 | tar -cJ -f /srv/backup/etc.tar.xz --null -T -`

C) `find /etc -type f | tar -cJ -f /srv/backup/etc.tar.xz --null -T -`

D) `find /etc -type f | tar -cJ -f /srv/backup/etc.tar.xz -null -T -`

Explanation

The `-print0` option for `find` and `--null` option for `tar` are used to handle filenames with spaces correctly.

Question 19:

Instead of opening a new remote shell session, command `ssh` can just execute a command indicated as its argument: `ssh user@storage "remote command"`. Given that `ssh` also allows to redirect the standard output of a local program to the standard input of the remote program, how would the `cat` command pipe a local file named `etc.tar.gz` to `/srv/backup/etc.tar.gz` at `user@storage` through `ssh`?

A) `cat etc.tar.gz | ssh user@storage "cat > /srv/backup/etc.tar.gz"`

((**Correct**))

B) `ssh user@storage "cat etc.tar.gz > /srv/backup/etc.tar.gz"`

C) `ssh user@storage "cat < etc.tar.gz > /srv/backup/etc.tar.gz"`

D) `cat etc.tar.gz > ssh user@storage "/srv/backup/etc.tar.gz"`

Explanation

This command pipes the contents of `etc.tar.gz` to `ssh`, which then executes `cat` to write the data to `/srv/backup/

etc.tar.gz` on the remote server.

Question 20:

Changing process priorities is usually required when a process is occupying too much CPU time. Using ps with standard options for printing all system processes in long format, what --sort flag will sort processes by CPU utilization, increasing order?

A) %cpu

((**Correct**))

B) %mem

C) time

D) pid

Explanation

The "--sort %cpu" flag will sort processes by CPU utilization in increasing order, allowing identification of processes consuming excessive CPU time.

Question 21:

Command schedtool can set all CPU scheduling parameters Linux is capable of or display information for given processes. How can it be used to display the scheduling parameters of process 1750? Also, how can schedtool be used to change process 1750 to real-time with priority -90 (as displayed by top)?

A) `schedtool -t -90 1750` to change priority, `schedtool -p 1750` to display parameters

B) `schedtool -p 1750` to display parameters, `schedtool -t

-90 1750` to change priority

((**Correct**))

C) `schedtool -a 1750` to display parameters, `schedtool -r -90 1750` to change priority

D) `schedtool -s 1750` to display parameters, `schedtool -r -90 1750` to change priority

Explanation

The command `schedtool -p 1750` is used to display the scheduling parameters of process 1750, while `schedtool -t -90 1750` is used to change its priority to real-time with a priority of -90.

Question 22:

The basic structure of an HTML file starts with elements html, head, and body. Describe how addresses could be used in sed to display only the body element and its contents.

A) `sed -n '/<html>/,/<\/html>/p' filename.html`

B) `sed -n '/<body>/,/<\/body>/p' filename.html`

((**Correct**))

C) `sed -n '/<head>/,/<\/head>/p' filename.html`

D) `sed -n '/<title>/,/<\/title>/p' filename.html`

Explanation

This sed command searches for the starting tag `<body>` and ending tag `</body>` in the HTML file and prints all lines between them, effectively displaying only the body element and its contents.

Question 23:

What sed expression will remove all tags from an HTML document, keeping only the rendered text?

A) `sed -e 's/<[^>]*>//g' filename.html`

((**Correct**))

B) `sed -e 's/<html>//g' filename.html`

C) `sed -e 's/<body>//g' filename.html`

D) `sed -e 's/<title>//g' filename.html`

Explanation

This sed command searches for any text within angle brackets `< >` and removes them, effectively stripping all HTML tags from the document.

Question 24:

What keys should be pressed in vi normal mode to delete characters from the current cursor position until the next period character?

A) `d.`

B) `d/`

C) `dt.`

((**Correct**))

D) `d)`

Explanation

Pressing `dt.` in normal mode will delete characters from the current cursor position until the next period character.

Question 25:

Which command is used to create a read-only snapshot of a Btrfs filesystem?

A) btrfs subvolume freeze

B) btrfs subvolume snapshot

((**Correct**))

C) btrfs subvolume backup

D) btrfs subvolume clone

Explanation

The btrfs subvolume snapshot command is used to create snapshots of a Btrfs filesystem.

Question 26:

What is the purpose of transparent file compression in Btrfs filesystem?

A) To increase disk space usage

B) To reduce disk space usage

((**Correct**))

C) To improve disk read/write speeds

D) To encrypt files on disk

Explanation

Transparent file compression in Btrfs filesystem helps to reduce disk space usage by compressing files automatically.

Question 27:

Which utility is used to create a swap partition on Linux?

A) mkswap

((**Correct**))

B) fdisk

C) parted

D) mkfs.ext4

Explanation

The mkswap utility is used to set up a swap partition on Linux.

Question 28:

What would happen to the ext2 filesystem /dev/sdb1 if the command below is issued? `tune2fs -j /dev/sdb1 -J device=/dev/sdc1 -i 30d`

A) It would be converted to ext3.

B) The journal would be moved to /dev/sdc1.

((**Correct**))

C) The filesystem would be checked for errors every 30 days.

D) It would be converted to ext4.

Explanation

The `-J device=/dev/sdc1` option moves the journal to the specified device, effectively converting the filesystem to ext3.

Question 29:

How can we check for errors on a XFS filesystem on /dev/sda1 that has a log section on /dev/sdc1, without actually making any repairs?

A) `xfs_check -n /dev/sda1`

((**Correct**))

B) `xfs_repair -n /dev/sda1`

C) `xfs_admin -n /dev/sda1`

D) `xfs_db -n /dev/sda1`

Explanation

The `xfs_check -n /dev/sda1` command checks for errors on the XFS filesystem without making any repairs, which is indicated by the `-n` option.

Question 30:

What is the difference between the -T and -t parameters for df?

A) -T displays the total disk space, while -t displays the filesystem type.

B) -T displays the filesystem type, while -t displays the total disk space.

((**Correct**))

C) -T displays the total number of inodes, while -t displays the total disk space.

D) -T displays the filesystem type, while -t displays the filesystem name.

Explanation

The `-T` option in `df` displays the filesystem type, while the `-t` option filters the output based on the filesystem type.

Question 31:

Consider the following entry in /etc/fstab: `/dev/sdc1 /backup ext4 noatime,nouser,async`. Can a user mount this filesystem with the command `mount /backup`? Why?

A) Yes, because `noauto` is not specified.

B) No, because `nouser` prevents regular users from mounting it.

((**Correct**))

C) Yes, because `async` overrides `nouser`.

D) No, because `ext4` filesystems cannot be mounted by users.

Explanation

The `nouser` option in `/etc/fstab` prevents regular users from mounting the filesystem. Therefore, users cannot mount it with the `mount /backup` command.

Question 32:

Write an /etc/fstab entry that would mount a btrfs volume with the label Backup on /mnt/backup, with default options and without allowing the execution of binaries from it.

A) `/dev/sdb1 /mnt/backup btrfs defaults,noexec`

B) `LABEL=Backup /mnt/backup btrfs defaults,noexec`

((**Correct**))

C) `UUID=<UUID> /mnt/backup btrfs defaults,noexec`

D) `/dev/disk/by-label/Backup /mnt/backup btrfs defaults,noexec`

Explanation

This entry mounts the btrfs volume labeled "Backup" at /mnt/backup with default options and the `noexec` flag to prevent the execution of binaries from the filesystem.

Question 33:

A system administrator wants to try different parameters for the bluetooth kernel module without rebooting the system. However, any attempt to unload the module with `modprobe -r bluetooth` results in the following error: `modprobe: FATAL: Module bluetooth is in use.` What is the possible cause for this error?

A) Another process is actively using the Bluetooth module.

((**Correct**))

B) The module is not installed correctly.

C) The module is required by the system for essential functions.

D) The administrator does not have sufficient permissions to unload the module.

Explanation

The error message indicates that the Bluetooth module cannot be unloaded because it is currently in use by another process, such as a Bluetooth service or application.

Question 34:

What is the symbolic mode representation for granting read and execute permissions to the owner of a file?

A) u+rx

((**Correct**))

B) o+rx

C) g+rx

D) a+rx

Explanation

In symbolic mode, `u+rx` grants read and execute permissions to the owner of a file.

Question 35:

How can you view hidden files when using the `ls` command?

A) Use the `-h` option.

B) Use the `-s` option.

C) Use the `-a` option.

((**Correct**))

D) Use the `-l` option.

Explanation

The `-a` option with the `ls` command is used to view hidden files.

Question 36:

Try this on a terminal: create an empty file called emptyfile with the command touch emptyfile. Now "zero out" the permissions for the file with chmod 000 emptyfile. What will happen if you change the permissions for emptyfile by passing only one value for chmod in octal mode, like chmod 4 emptyfile? And if you use two, as in chmod 44 emptyfile? What can we learn about the way chmod reads the numerical value?

A) Both commands will make the file non-executable.

((**Correct**))

B) The first command will make the file readable, and the second one will make it writable.

C) The first command will set the permissions to 004 (read-only for others), and the second one will set them to 044 (read-write for group).

D) Both commands will produce an error.

Explanation

The first digit in the octal notation represents the owner's permissions, the second digit represents the group's permissions, and the third digit represents others' permissions. Therefore, using only one digit like `4` or `44` sets the permissions accordingly. Since there's no `x` for any user, the file becomes non-executable.

Question 37:

Consider the permissions for the temporary directory on a Linux system, /tmp: `drwxrwxrwt 19 root root 16K Dec 21 18:58 tmp`. User, group and others have full permissions. But can a regular user delete any files inside this directory? Why is this the case?

A) Yes, because of the sticky bit.

((**Correct**))

B) No, because of the sticky bit.

C) Yes, because the directory is owned by root.

D) No, because the directory is owned by root.

Explanation

The sticky bit (`t`) set on a directory restricts users from deleting files they don't own, even if they have write permissions on the directory. However, the owner of a file can always delete their own files regardless of the sticky bit.

Question 38:

How would you create a directory named Box where all the files are automatically owned by the group users, and can only be deleted by the user who created them?

A) `mkdir Box && chmod g+s,o+t Box`

((**Correct**))

B) `mkdir Box && chmod u+s,o+t Box`

C) `mkdir Box && chmod g+s,u+t Box`

D) `mkdir Box && chmod u+s,g+t Box`

Explanation

The command `mkdir Box` creates the directory, and `chmod g+s,o+t Box` sets the setgid bit (`g+s`) to make all files created within the directory inherit the group ownership, and the sticky bit (`o+t`) to prevent users from deleting files they don't own.

Question 39:

Indicate if the following statements/features correspond to GNU Screen, tmux, or both:

N| Feature/Statement: | GNU Screen | tmux |

1| Default command prefix is Ctrl + a | Y | Y |

2| Client-Server Model | Y | Y |

3| Panes are pseudo-terminals | Y | Y |

4| Killing a region does not kill its associated window(s) | N | Y |

5| Sessions include windows | Y | Y |

6| Sessions can be detached | Y | Y |

True

((**Correct**))

False

Explanation:

1. Default command prefix is Ctrl + a: Both GNU Screen and tmux use Ctrl + a as the default command prefix, allowing users to send commands to the multiplexer.

2. Client-Server Model: Both GNU Screen and tmux follow the client-server model, where a single instance of the multiplexer acts as a server managing multiple client sessions.

3. Panes are pseudo-terminals: Both GNU Screen and tmux

utilize panes as pseudo-terminals, allowing users to split the terminal window into multiple independent sections.

4. Killing a region does not kill its associated window(s):

4.1 GNU Screen: In GNU Screen, killing a region also kills its associated window(s). Therefore, the statement is marked as "N" for GNU Screen.

4.2 tmux: In tmux, killing a region does not kill its associated window(s). Therefore, the statement is marked as "Y" for tmux.

5. Sessions include windows: Both GNU Screen and tmux organize terminal sessions into windows, which are included within each session.

6. Sessions can be detached: Both GNU Screen and tmux allow users to detach from sessions, allowing them to disconnect from the terminal while keeping the session running in the background.

Therefore, the correct answers for each statement/feature are:

1. Default command prefix is Ctrl + a: Both GNU Screen and tmux (Y)

2. Client-Server Model: Both GNU Screen and tmux (Y)

3. Panes are pseudo-terminals: Both GNU Screen and tmux (Y)

4. Killing a region does not kill its associated window(s):

4.1 GNU Screen: No (N)

4.2 tmux: Yes (Y)

5. Sessions include windows: Both GNU Screen and tmux (Y)

6. Sessions can be detached: Both GNU Screen and tmux (Y)

Question 40:

Install GNU Screen on your computer (package name: screen) and complete the following tasks:

1. Start the program. What command do you use?

A) `screen`

B) `screen -S session_name`

C) `start-screen`

D) `open-screen`

2. Start top:

A) Press `Ctrl + a`, then `:`, then type `screen top`

B) Press `Ctrl + a`, then `c`

C) Press `Ctrl + a`, then `:`, then type `top`

D) Press `Ctrl + a`, then `top`

3. Using screen's key prefix, open a new window; then, open /etc/screenrc using vi:

A) Press `Ctrl + a`, then `c`, then type `vi /etc/screenrc`

B) Press `Ctrl + a`, then `:`, then type `new`, then press `Enter`, then type `vi /etc/screenrc`

C) Press `Ctrl + a`, then `:`, then type `new`, then press `Enter`, then type `screen /etc/screenrc`

D) Press `Ctrl + a`, then `:`, then type `vi /etc/screenrc`

4. List the windows at the bottom of the screen:

A) Press `Ctrl + a`, then `w`

B) Press `Ctrl + a`, then `:`, then type `list`, then press `Enter`

C) Press `Ctrl + a`, then `:`, then type `windows`, then press `Enter`

D) Press `Ctrl + a`, then `list`

5. Change the name of the current window to vi:

A) Press `Ctrl + a`, then `:`, then type `title vi`, then press `Enter`

B) Press `Ctrl + a`, then `A`, then type `vi`, then press `Enter`

C) Press `Ctrl + a`, then `:`, then type `rename vi`, then press `Enter`

D) Press `Ctrl + a`, then `:`, then type `title vi`

6. Change the name of the remaining window to top. To do that, first display a list of all windows so that you can move up and down and select the right one:

A) Press `Ctrl + a`, then `:`, then type `title top`, then press `Enter`

B) Press `Ctrl + a`, then `:`, then type `rename top`, then press `Enter`

C) Press `Ctrl + a`, then `n`, then type `top`, then press `Enter`

D) Press `Ctrl + a`, then `:`, then type `rename 2 top`, then press `Enter`

7. Check that the names have changed by having the window names displayed at the bottom of the screen again:

A) Press `Ctrl + a`, then `w`

B) Press `Ctrl + a`, then `:`, then type `list`, then press `Enter`

C) Press `Ctrl + a`, then `:`, then type `windows`, then press `Enter`

D) Press `Ctrl + a`, then `list`

8. Now, detach the session and have screen create a new one named ssh:

A) Press `Ctrl + a`, then `d`, then `screen -S ssh`

B) Press `Ctrl + a`, then `:`, then type `detach`, then press `Enter`, then type `screen -S ssh`

C) Press `Ctrl + a`, then `d`, then `ssh`

D) Press `Ctrl + a`, then `:`, then type `detach`, then press `Enter`, then type `ssh`

9. Detach also from ssh and have screen display the list of sessions:

A) Press `Ctrl + a`, then `:`, then type `list`, then press `Enter`

B) Press `Ctrl + a`, then `ls`, then press `Enter`

C) Press `Ctrl + a`, then `:`, then type `sessions`, then press `Enter`

D) Press `Ctrl + a`, then `s`

10. Now, attach to the first session using its PID:

A) `screen -r <PID>`

B) `screen -x <PID>`

C) `screen -a <PID>`

D) `screen -S <PID>`

11. You should be back at the window displaying top. Split the window horizontally and move to the new empty region:

A) Press `Ctrl + a`, then `:`, then type `split`, then press `Enter`, then `Ctrl + a`, then `TAB`, then `Ctrl + a`, then `c`

B) Press `Ctrl + a`, then `:` then type `split`, then press `Enter`, then `Ctrl + a`, then `TAB`, then `Ctrl + a`, then `c`

C) Press `Ctrl + a`, then `Shift + s`, then `Ctrl + a`, then `TAB`, then `Ctrl + a`, then `c`

D) Press `Ctrl + a`, then `c`, then `Ctrl + a`, then `:`, then type `split`, then press `Enter`

12. Have screen list all windows and select vi to be displayed in the new empty region:

A) Press `Ctrl + a`, then `w`, then type `vi`, then press `Enter`

B) Press `Ctrl + a`, then `:`, then type `select vi`, then press `Enter`

C) Press `Ctrl + a`, then `:`, then type `window vi`, then press `Enter`

D) Press `Ctrl + a`, then `"` (double quotation mark), then type `vi`, then press `Enter`

13. Now, split the current region vertically, move into the newly created empty region and associate it with a brand new window:

A) Press `Ctrl + a`, then `:` then type `split -v`, then press `Enter`, then `Ctrl + a`, then `TAB`, then `Ctrl + a`, then `c`

B) Press `Ctrl + a`, then `|`, then `Ctrl + a`, then `TAB`, then `Ctrl + a`, then `c`

C) Press `Ctrl + a`, then `Shift + |` (vertical bar), then `Ctrl + a`, then `TAB`, then `Ctrl + a`, then `c`

D) Press `Ctrl + a`, then `:`, then type `split -h`, then press `Enter`, then `Ctrl + a`, then `TAB`, then `Ctrl + a`, then `c`

14. Terminate all regions except the current one (remember, although you kill the regions, the windows are still alive). Then, quit out of all the windows of the current session until the session itself is terminated:

A) Press `Ctrl + a`, then `:`, then type `killall`, then press `Enter`, then press `y` for confirmation

B) Press `Ctrl + a`, then `:`, then type `kill -`, then press `Enter`, then press `y` for confirmation

C) Press `Ctrl + a`, then `:`, then type `killall but this`, then press `Enter`, then press `y` for confirmation

D) Press `Ctrl + a`, then `:`, then type `quit`, then press `Enter`, then press `y` for confirmation

15. Finally, have the screen list its sessions one more time, kill the remaining ssh session by PID, and check that there are no sessions left:

A) Press `Ctrl + a`, then `:`, then type `sessions`, then press `Enter`, then type `kill <PID>`, then press `Enter`

B) Press `Ctrl + a`, then `:`, then type `ls`, then press `Enter`, then type `kill <PID>`, then press `Enter`

C) Press `Ctrl + a`, then `:` then type `list`, then press

`Enter`, then type `kill -S <PID>`, then press `Enter`

D) Press `Ctrl + a`, then `s`, then type `kill -9 <PID>`, then press `Enter`

1. A), 2. C), 3. B), 4. A), 5. A), 6. D), 7. A), 8. B), 9. A), 10. A), 11. C), 12. D), 13. A), 14. A), 15. C)

((**Correct**))

1. C), 2. A), 3. C), 4. B), 5. A), 6. A), 7. D), 8. A), 9. B), 10. A), 11. A), 12. C), 13. D), 14. A), 15. A)

1. D), 2. A), 3. C), 4. B), 5. A), 6. A), 7. A), 8. B), 9. A), 10. A), 11. C), 12. D), 13. A), 14. A), 15. C)

1. A), 2. B), 3. A), 4. C), 5. B), 6. A), 7. A), 8. D), 9. A), 10. A), 11. C), 12. D), 13. A), 14. A), 15. C)

Question 41:

Consider the following systemd mount unit:

[Unit]

Description=External data disk

[Mount]

What=/dev/disk/by-uuid/56C11DCC5D2E1334

Where=/mnt/external

Type=ntfs

Options=defaults

[Install]

WantedBy=multi-user.target

What would be an equivalent /etc/fstab entry for this filesystem?

A) `/dev/disk/by-uuid/56C11DCC5D2E1334 /mnt/external ntfs defaults 0 0`

((**Correct**))

B) `UUID=56C11DCC5D2E1334 /mnt/external ntfs defaults 0 0`

C) `/mnt/external /dev/disk/by-uuid/56C11DCC5D2E1334 ntfs defaults 0 0`

D) `/mnt/external UUID=56C11DCC5D2E1334 ntfs defaults 0 0`

Explanation

This entry specifies the device's UUID, mount point, filesystem type, mount options, and dump and fsck options, which are the components of an /etc/fstab entry.

Question 42:

Consider the following 4 files:

Another_Directory: drwxr-xr-t

foo.bar: ----r--r--

HugeFile.zip: -rw-rw-r--

Sample_Directory: drwxr-sr-x

Write down the corresponding permissions for each file and directory using octal mode using the 4-digit notation.

1. Another_Directory: 1755, foo.bar: 0444, HugeFile.zip: 0664, Sample_Directory: 2755

((**Correct**))

2. Another_Directory: 1744, foo.bar: 0222, HugeFile.zip: 0774, Sample_Directory: 5755

3. Another_Directory: 1722, foo.bar: 0555, HugeFile.zip: 0664, Sample_Directory: 4755

4. Another_Directory: 1775, foo.bar: 0444, HugeFile.zip: 0554, Sample_Directory: 2755

Explanation

To convert the symbolic notation of file permissions to octal mode using the 4-digit notation, we need to understand the meaning of each symbol in the symbolic notation:

d: Represents a directory.

r: Indicates read permission.

w: Indicates write permission.

x: Indicates execute permission.

t: Indicates the sticky bit is set.

s: Indicates the setuid or setgid bit is set.

Using this information, let's convert each file's permissions:

Another_Directory: drwxr-xr-t

drwxr-xr-t translates to 1755 in octal mode.

foo.bar: ----r--r--

----r--r-- translates to 0444 in octal mode.

HugeFile.zip: -rw-rw-r--

-rw-rw-r-- translates to 0664 in octal mode.

Sample_Directory: drwxr-sr-x

drwxr-sr-x translates to 2755 in octal mode.

Therefore, the correct answer is option 1:

Another_Directory: 1755

foo.bar: 0444

HugeFile.zip: 0664

Sample_Directory: 2755

Question 43:

Which of the following commands is used to display the current directory in Linux?

A) ls

B) pwd

(**(Correct)**)

C) cd

D) cat

Explanation

The `pwd` command stands for "print working directory" and is used to display the current working directory in Linux.

Question 44:

What is the purpose of the `chmod` command in Linux?

A) Change ownership of files

B) Change file permissions

((**Correct**))

C) Change file timestamps

D) Change file contents

Explanation

The `chmod` command is used to change the permissions (read, write, execute) of files and directories in Linux.

Question 45:

Which of the following commands is used to list all currently running processes in Linux?

A) ps

((**Correct**))

B) top

C) ls

D) grep

Explanation

The `ps` command is used to list currently running processes in Linux.

Question 46:

What does the acronym "CLI" stand for in the context of Linux?

A) Command Line Interpreter

B) Common Language Interface

C) Command Line Interface

((**Correct**))

D) Common Line Instruction

Explanation

CLI stands for Command Line Interface, which is a text-based interface used to interact with the operating system by typing commands.

Question 47:

Which of the following commands is used to create a new directory in Linux?

A) mkdir

((**Correct**))

B) touch

C) mv

D) rm

Explanation

The `mkdir` command is used to create a new directory in Linux.

Question 48:

Which of the following commands would display the current CPU architecture of your Linux system?

A) cat /proc/cpuinfo

B) arch

C) lscpu

((**Correct**))

D) uname -p

Explanation

cat /proc/cpuinfo provides detailed information about the CPU, but not summarized architecture.

arch is a similar command to uname -p, but less standardized across distributions.

uname -p shows general processor type, not always the specific architecture.

lscpu is dedicated to providing a clear and concise summary of CPU architecture information.

Question 49:

You need to install a software package that is not available in your Linux distribution's default repositories. You've located a .rpm package file for the software. Which tool should you use for installation?

A) apt-get

B) yum

C) dpkg

D) rpm

((**Correct**))

Explanation

apt-get is used on Debian-based systems (Ubuntu, etc.)

yum is used on older Red Hat-based systems (RHEL, CentOS).

Newer versions often use dnf.

dpkg is a lower-level tool used on Debian-based systems

rpm is the Red Hat Package Manager, designed to work directly with .rpm files.

Question 50:

You want to view the contents of a file named "report.txt", but display it one screenful at a time. Which command should you use?

A) cat report.txt

B) tail report.txt

C) less report.txt

((**Correct**))

D) head report.txt

Explanation

cat report.txt dumps the entire file contents to the screen at once.

tail report.txt shows the last few lines of the file.

head report.txt shows the first few lines of the file.

less report.txt allows you to page through the file, navigate up/down, and search.

Question 51:

In the Linux filesystem hierarchy, which directory typically contains configuration files for system-wide services?

A) /home

B) /etc

((**Correct**))

C) /var

D) /usr

Explanation

/home contains users' home directories.

/etc houses system-wide configuration files.

/var contains variable data like logs, databases, etc.

/usr contains binaries, libraries, and other non-modifiable system files.

Question 52:

Which of the following commands will write a message to the terminals of all logged in users?

A) bcast

B) mesg

C) write

D) wall

((**Correct**))

Explanation

The wall command in Linux is used to send a message to all users in a terminal session. The mesg command is used to control write access to your terminal, write is used to send a message to another user, and bcast is not a valid command.

Question 53:

Which of the following commands can be used to search for the executable file corresponding to a given command?

A) find

B) locate

C) which

((**Correct**))

D) whereis

Explanation

The which command in Linux is used to locate the executable file associated with the given command. It returns the path of the executable that would have been executed when this command is run. The find and locate commands can also find files, but they do not specifically find executable files. The whereis command locates the binary, source, and manual page files for a command, but it does not necessarily return the executable that would have been run.

Question 54:

Which of the following commands will display the current directory?

A) ls

B) dir

C) pwd

((**Correct**))

D) cd

Explanation

The pwd command in Linux stands for 'print working directory', and when executed, it prints the current directory. The ls and dir commands list the contents of a directory, and the cd command is used to change the current directory.

Question 55:

Which command would you use to display information about the user currently logged in?

A) id

((**Correct**))

B) whoami

C) sudo -i

D) su

Explanation

id displays user and group information for the current user.

whoami simply displays the current username.

sudo -i and su are commands to switch users, not display information.

Question 56:

You have a script that needs to check if a file exists. Which command would you use inside the script for this purpose?

A) if [-f file.txt]

((**Correct**))

B) test -e file.txt

C) find file.txt

D) locate file.txt

Explanation

[-f file.txt] is a conditional statement to check if "file.txt" is a regular file.

test -e file.txt achieves the same functionality.

find file.txt searches for the file, not specifically checking if it exists.

locate file.txt uses the locate database to search, not ideal for checking existence.

Question 57:

Which command would you use to view your system's current IP address?

A) uname -n

B) hostname

C) ip addr

((**Correct**))

D) ifconfig

Explanation

uname -n displays the hostname, not the IP address.

hostname displays the hostname, not the IP address.

ip addr (or ifconfig) shows network interface details, including IP addresses.

Question 58:

What is the primary purpose of file permissions in Linux?

A) To determine system uptime

B) To manage user and group access to files and directories

((**Correct**))

C) To track file modifications

D) To assign ownership of files

Explanation

File permissions control who (owner, group, others) can read, write, and execute files/directories.

System uptime is not directly related to file permissions.

While permissions can track ownership, that's not their primary function.

Ownership is one factor in determining permissions, but not the sole purpose.

Question 59:

A service on your Linux system is not starting. Which command can you use to check the service logs for potential errors?

A) cat /var/log/messages

B) journalctl -u servicename

((**Correct**))

C) dmesg

D) ps aux

Explanation

/var/log/messages might contain service-related logs, but it's not specific.

journalctl -u servicename allows you to view logs specific to the service by name.

dmesg primarily shows kernel logs.

ps aux displays running processes, not helpful for analyzing service logs.

Question 60:

During the Linux boot process, which of the following is NOT typically loaded before reaching the init system?

A) Kernel modules

B) Device drivers

C) User applications

((**Correct**))

D) File system drivers

Explanation

Kernel modules, device drivers, and file system drivers are essential for basic system functionality and typically load before the init system.

User applications launch after the login prompt appears, handled by the init system.

EPILOGUE

Congratulations! You've reached the end of this comprehensive guide to the LPIC-1 101-500 V5 exam. By diligently working through the practice exams, mastering the key concepts, and leveraging the provided resources, you've equipped yourself with the knowledge and skills necessary to excel in the exam.

Remember, the LPIC-1 certification is just the first step on your journey to becoming a skilled Linux administrator. The world of Linux is vast and ever-evolving. Embrace the continuous learning mindset, stay curious, and keep exploring. Here are some ways to stay engaged:

- **Join online communities and forums:** Connect with other Linux enthusiasts and professionals to share knowledge, ask questions, and collaborate on projects.
- **Contribute to open-source projects:** Immerse yourself in the open-source spirit by contributing to existing projects or even starting your own.
- **Stay updated on the latest trends and technologies:** The Linux landscape is constantly evolving, so make it a habit to stay informed about new developments and emerging tools.
- **Pursue further certifications:** As your knowledge and skills grow, consider exploring advanced Linux certifications to further enhance your career prospects.

The key to success in this field lies in your passion for learning and your commitment to continuous improvement. I wish you the very best of luck in your LPIC-1 exam and your future endeavors in the exciting realm of Linux administration!

ABOUT THE AUTHOR

Ghada Atef: A Passionate Linux Pro

Ghada Atef, a seasoned Linux expert, is deeply passionate about open-source technologies. Her expertise spans various Linux distributions and their practical applications. She has authored a range of valuable resources to empower aspiring Linux professionals:

1. “RHCSA 9 (EX200) Exam Prep”: The third edition of this comprehensive guide features six complete practice exams for the RHCSA 9 (EX200) certification.
2. “Mastering Ansible”: Dive into the world of Ansible with practical insights on automating configuration management and deployment.
3. “Ubuntu Mastery”: Ghada’s in-depth guide to mastering Ubuntu, one of the most popular Linux distributions.
4. “RHCSA 8 & 9 Exam Prep”: A thorough preparation guide for the RHCSA 8 & 9 (EX200) exam, including six practice exams.
5. “RHCE EX294 Mastery”: Detailed answers and strategies to excel in the Red Hat Certified Engineer EX294 Exam.
6. “Confident RHCSA 9 (EX200) Prep”: An online course designed to boost confidence and knowledge for the RHCSA 9 (EX200) exam.

Ghada’s work stands out for its practical approach, clear

explanations, and real-world relevance. Whether you're a beginner or a seasoned pro, her books and courses are invaluable resources on your Linux journey.

BOOKS BY THIS AUTHOR

Unofficial Rhcsa 8 & 9 (Ex200) Complete Reference: Rhel 8 & 9

"Unofficial RHCSA 8 & 9 (EX200) Complete Reference: RHEL 8 & 9" is a comprehensive guide that covers all the topics and objectives of the Red Hat Certified System Administrator (RHCSA) exam for RHEL 8 and 9. Whether you're a beginner or an experienced Linux user, this book provides you with the knowledge and skills to become proficient in managing and maintaining RHEL systems. From installation and configuration to system management, networking, security, and troubleshooting, this book covers everything you need to know to pass the RHCSA exam and become a certified system administrator. With clear explanations, practical examples, and real-world scenarios, "Unofficial RHCSA 8 & 9 (EX200) Complete Reference: RHEL 8 & 9" is an essential resource for anyone preparing for the RHCSA exam or seeking to improve their RHEL skills.

Mastering Ansible: A Comprehensive Guide To Automating Configuration Management And Deployment

"Mastering Ansible: A Comprehensive Guide to Automating Configuration Management and Deployment" is an in-depth guide to Ansible, a popular open-source tool for automating infrastructure as code.

The book covers everything from the basics of Ansible to advanced topics such as modules, plugins, roles, and dynamic inventory. It provides detailed guidance on how to write efficient, modular, and reusable playbooks, and how to use Ansible to automate a wide range of tasks, from provisioning servers to deploying applications.

The book also includes best practices, tips, and tricks for working effectively with Ansible, as well as use cases and real-world examples.

Whether you're a beginner or an experienced user, "Mastering Ansible" will help you become a master of Ansible and take your automation skills to the next level.

Unofficial Red Hat Certified Engineer (Rhce) Ex294 Exam Guide: A Comprehensive Study Resource For Red Hat Enterprise Linux 9

Looking to become a Red Hat Certified Engineer (RHCE)? Look no further than "Unofficial Red Hat Certified Engineer (RHCE) EX294 Exam Guide"! This comprehensive study resource is designed to help you pass the RHCE EX294 exam with ease, providing in-depth coverage of all exam objectives and six complete practice exams to help you sharpen your skills. With its clear explanations, helpful tips, and real-world scenarios, this book is an essential tool for anyone looking to succeed on the RHCE EX294 exam and take their Linux skills to the next level. So why wait? Get your copy today and start preparing for exam success!

Mastering Ubuntu: A Comprehensive Guide To Linux's Favorite Distribution

Looking to master one of the most popular Linux distributions around? Look no further than "Mastering Ubuntu"! This comprehensive guide takes you on a journey from beginner to expert, with step-by-step tutorials and practical examples to help you get the most out of your Ubuntu system. Whether you're a developer, sysadmin, or just a curious user, "Mastering Ubuntu" has everything you need to take your skills to the next level. From installation and configuration to networking, security, and beyond, this book is your ultimate resource for mastering Ubuntu.

Learn Pycharm Ide For Kids: Using Pycharm Python Ide Community Edition

Looking for a fun and engaging way to introduce your child to the world of programming? Look no further than "Learn PyCharm IDE for Kids: Using PyCharm Python IDE Community Edition." This book offers a comprehensive guide to the PyCharm Python IDE, one of the most popular tools for programming in Python. With clear and easy-to-follow instructions, your child will learn how to use PyCharm to write and run Python code, as well as how to debug and troubleshoot their programs. Whether your child is a complete beginner or has some programming experience, "Learn PyCharm IDE for Kids" is the perfect resource to help them take their coding skills to the next level.

Unofficial Red Hat Rhcsa 9 (Ex200) Exam Preparation 2023: Six Complete Rhcsa 9 (Ex200) Practice Exams With Answers (Third Edition)

Looking to ace the Red Hat RHCSA 9 (EX200) exam? Look no further than the "Unofficial Red Hat RHCSA 9 (EX200) Exam Preparation 2023" book. With six complete practice exams for RHCSA 9, this book is the ultimate study resource for anyone preparing to take the RHCSA exam. Whether you're a beginner or an experienced professional, these practice exams will test your knowledge and skills, giving you the confidence you need to pass the RHCSA exam with flying colors. With answers and detailed explanations included, you'll be able to review and strengthen your understanding of key concepts, commands, and techniques. Don't take the RHCSA exam without this essential study guide!

Rhce Ex294 Mastery: Six Practice Exams For Exam Success

This book, "RHCE EX294 Mastery: Six Practice Exams for Exam Success," is your comprehensive guide to achieving RHCE certification. It provides the tools, strategies, and in-depth knowledge to confidently ace the RHCE EX294 exam and establish yourself as a true RHEL expert.

Command Line Mastery

A Comprehensive Guide to Linux and Bash: 615 MCQs with detailed explanations on Filesystem, Process Management, Permissions, Networking, and Bash Scripting

THANK YOU!

www.ingramcontent.com/pod-product-compliance
Lightning Source LLC
LaVergne TN
LVHW051221050326
832903LV00028B/2199

* 9 7 9 8 8 8 3 0 8 4 7 3 6 *